PRICELESS

by

Lloyd Constantine

PUBLISHING

New York

Published by Kaplan Publishing, a division of Kaplan, Inc.
1 Liberty Plaza, 24th Floor
New York, NY 10006

Library of Congress Cataloging-in-Publication Data

Constantine, Lloyd.
Priceless : the case that brought down the Visa/Mastercard bank cartel / Lloyd Constantine.
   p. cm.
ISBN 978-1-60714-468-7
1. Wal-Mart (Firm)--Trials, litigation, etc. 2. VISA U.S.A., Inc.--Trials, litigation, etc. 3. MasterCard International Incorporated--Trials, litigation, etc. 4. Point-of-sale systems industry--Law and legislation--United States. 5. Antitrust law--United States. 6. Credit cards--Law and legislation-- United States. 7. Debit cards--Law and legislation--United States. 8. Stored-value cards--Law and legislation--United States. I. Title.
KF229.W35C66 2009
343.73'0721--dc22

                            2009023223

Printed in the United States of America

10 9 8 7 6 5 4 3 2 1

ISBN: 978-1-60714-456-4

Kaplan Publishing books are available at special quantity discounts to use for sales promotions, employee premiums, or educational purposes. Please email our Special Sales Department to order or for more information at kaplanpublishing@kaplan.com, or write to Kaplan Publishing, 1 Liberty Plaza, 24th Floor, New York, NY 10006.

This book and the work it chronicles are dedicated to

Jan, Isaac, Sarah, Elizabeth, "Connie," and Edna.

They are the reason for my life.

TABLE OF CONTENTS

An Expensive Dinner
for MasterCard

———

THE NIGHT OF JULY 10, 1989, I hosted a buffet dinner at my Manhattan apartment for my fellow assistant attorneys general from 14 states. Everyone assembled on West Sixty-Sixth Street for my mostly green banquet of chili, broccoli soup, salad, tabouleh and pasta with pesto. Although the get-together at my place was intended to be social, allowing me to show off my wife and kids and our views of Central Park and the Chagall windows of the Metropolitan Opera House to colleagues from cities like Baton Rouge and Austin, the dinner conversation was dominated by a discussion of the credit card giants, Visa and MasterCard, whose combined market share was more than 95 percent. These companies had announced the merger of their separate debit card networks, forming a new joint network called "Entrée." The general opinion was that this debit card merger was designed to dominate that fledgling but inevitably huge business and destroy competing debit card networks like NYCE, MAC, STAR and Shazam.

The 14 states had responded to the announcement of the merger with a letter stating their intent to sue Visa and MasterCard. As head of the Task Force that coordinated antitrust enforcement for all 50 states, I was lead counsel of the team. The investigation that had led up to that day had taken 16 months, and we were now ready to act. The lawsuit we would soon file against Visa and MasterCard was not merely the culmination of that 16-month probe, it was the tangible result of nearly a decade of work. That night, we talked about the progress that the states had made in our efforts to fill the void created by the virtual abdication of antitrust enforcement in the administration of President Ronald Reagan. Many of my dinner guests had participated in every step of this effort.

A full-day meeting with Visa had occurred that day, and a similar meeting with MasterCard was scheduled for the next day. Meetings like those we were holding with the bankcard associations are usually offered to target companies prior to civil suit or indictment. They rarely change anything but are used by both sides as an opportunity to learn something from the other side prior to formal hostilities. These particular meetings, however, wound up changing the entire course of dealings between me and the targets, and especially with MasterCard.

The meeting earlier that day with Visa had been polite, if inconsequential. Most of it had been consumed by Visa's substantially and sadly accurate explanation of how the symbiotic relationship between Visa and MasterCard and the lack of real competition between them was the product of antitrust enforcement decisions made by our counterparts in the federal Antitrust Division. By 1989, the antitrust laws had been sapped of much of their vitality. After eight years in which Reagan administration antitrust officials had systematically dismantled the enforcement agencies and waged a campaign in the Congress and courts to trivialize the law, state attorney general (AG) enforcement, which I coordnated, was the last and only line of defense. Visa predicted that if the state AGs were to try to break up the Entrée joint venture, we would fail—as the many previous antitrust suits against Visa and MasterCard had.

At 11:00 PM that night, after my dinner with the other Assistant AGs and hours before a scheduled meeting with MasterCard, Tim Cone, a young colleague, called to tell me about a conversation he had overheard at former baseball star Rusty Staub's new restaurant on Fifth Avenue. Tim, his fiancée Diana and his father Terry Cone, a senior partner at the Cleary Gottlieb law firm, heard three men discussing the meeting they were going to have with me the next day. The men said that an investigator would be hired to uncover something about me that I wouldn't want revealed and that they would threaten to expose me unless I laid off MasterCard.

From Tim's description, I was reasonably sure that one of the three men was Bob Norton, MasterCard's General Counsel, and that another was Stanley Robinson, a senior antitrust partner at the Kaye Scholer law firm. I told Tim that I didn't take the conversation seriously and considered it macho dinner bluster, perhaps fueled by alcohol. Tim put Terry Cone on the phone, who related the same story and told me that the discussion about the investigator had come in the middle of a sober, serious and straight-faced discussion of legal issues and tactics that would be used to defend MasterCard. He said he had practiced law for many years, knew what he had heard, and was positive that the men were serious about their plan to investigate and then threaten me.

I called my boss, New York Attorney General Bob Abrams, and we convened a midnight conference call with Bob, Mary Ellen Burns, the chief of the AG's Public Advocacy Division, and Jack Ryan, our chief of criminal prosecutions, who had skillfully conducted the highly publicized Tawana Brawley grand jury investigation, involving sensationalized allegations of sexual abuse and mistreatment of a teenage African-American girl by white police and prosecutors in an upstate New York community. We agreed that I should call back the Cones and ask whether they would identify the three men prior to the meeting. I also asked them immediately to memorialize the conversation they had overheard, without further discussing it. They agreed to do this. The Cones also told me that the men had agreed to walk out of the meeting at exactly 12:30 PM and say that there was "nothing more to discuss."

The next day, prior to the meeting, the three MasterCard lawyers were identified by Tim Cone, who was positioned behind a glass barrier where he could see, but not be seen from, inside the room where he was positioned. Then the meeting began. In contrast to the previous day's meeting with Visa, the session with MasterCard was aimless. The three MasterCard lawyers talked and joked with each other and broke four times in just two and one-half hours. At precisely 12:30 PM they got up, and Bob Norton said that the meeting was over, because there was "nothing further to discuss." I realized that the Cones were probably correct about what they had heard the night before.

According to a plan that we had established the previous night, I asked the MasterCard lawyers to speak with me privately and escorted them into Mary Ellen Burns's office, where she and Jack Ryan were waiting. Turning to Norton, now identified as the lawyer who had said I would be investigated and threatened, I asked if they had dined at Rusty Staub's restaurant the previous night.

"Yes," Norton said.

I asked Norton if he were hiring an investigator to try to uncover illegal or embarrassing activities I had or was engaged in. Norton unraveled. He just started talking: "Oh my God, Oh my God. I know you're not supposed to talk in bathrooms. I know you're not supposed to talk in elevators. I said it. I said it. But I didn't mean it! It was a joke. You've got to believe me, it was a joke! No matter what we found out about you, we wouldn't use it. If you used drugs, we wouldn't use it. If we found out about some weird sexual behavior, we wouldn't use it. No matter what, we wouldn't use it. Lloyd, you've got to believe me!"

Norton continued to rattle on about other illegal and embarrassing things they might uncover if they were to investigate me, which they wouldn't have, but in any event would never reveal about me. This went on for a while in a panicked stream of consciousness reminiscent of Sherman McCoy's confession in Tom Wolfe's *The Bonfire of the Vanities*. Stanley Robinson and the other MasterCard lawyer seemed paralyzed. Robinson finally said, "Bob, shut up."

I turned to Robinson, a man then in his late sixties and one of the big names in antitrust at the Kaye Scholer law firm, which then had one of the premier antitrust practices in the United States. I told him that if he wanted to know something about me, he didn't have to hire an investigator—he could just ask his law partner and my friend, Josh Greenberg, or Bob Kandel in his firm's real estate department, who was my classmate at both Williams College and Columbia Law School.

Robinson said, "You have to believe me, Lloyd, that I didn't think Bob was serious." I asked him what he had done to make sure that "Bob" wasn't serious. He did not answer.

I told Robinson I was distressed about where our profession was headed. "Stanley, ten years ago, if a client of yours had said something like this, you would have fired the client on the spot. And five years ago, you would have, at least, made sure that it was just talk. But now, you just assumed that it wasn't serious, without doing anything to make sure." I then said to all three, "Get out of our offices. I will figure out what I am going to do about you and about this." They literally ran out of the office.

That day, I got calls from several acquaintances at Kaye Scholer. They begged me not to take action against Stanley Robinson or their firm. Josh Greenberg, the head of Kay Scholer's antitrust department, told me that Robinson's career had been distinguished, full of good and charitable works, and that Robinson had been his mentor. Besides that, Josh added that Robinson was about to retire. In fact, Stanley Robinson would continue to practice and represent Master-Card for several years.

I called Hal Lieberman, the chief counsel of the Departmental Disciplinary Committee for New York's First Judicial Department in Manhattan. I told him about the incident, leaving out names. Realizing that I might be under some duty to report it to the disciplinary committee, I said the facts involved a friend of mine. Without directly saying so, Lieberman let me know that he understood that I was talking about myself. He said "my friend" was probably obliged under the disciplinary rules to report the incident to his office.

I thanked Hal for his advice and said I would pass it along to my friend. I did not, however, report Robert Norton, Stanley Robinson, or the incident. I believed that pressing an ethics complaint could make it difficult for me to litigate against MasterCard. This case was more important than putting some jerks in their place.

I was also just beginning to realize the magnitude of what would be involved in our attempts to break up the Entrée joint venture. The MasterCard incident reminded me of the infamous effort by General Motors to discredit Ralph Nader during his early crusade against the "unsafe at any speed" Chevy Corvair. MasterCard's discussion about discrediting me suggested that what we had discovered, in a relatively cursory investigation of Visa and MasterCard, was just the tip of an anticompetitive iceberg.

Moreover, the broader issues of what I considered to be the abandonment of antitrust enforcement by the Department of Justice and the abdication of the Federal Reserve's stewardship of the U.S. payment system and its privatization by the Visa/MasterCard bank cartel, was a matter of great importance to the economy of the country. Like their colleagues at the federal antitrust agencies, the Reagan-Bush officials at the Fed were fanatical believers that the market would cure everything and always deliver optimal results. So, as electronic debit card transactions started to replace paper checks and cash, the Fed had begun to abandon its traditional role of regulating the nation's payment system. The result was a great transfer of wealth from stores and consumers into the pockets of the banks and Visa/MasterCard.

I swallowed my private anger against MasterCard and proceeded in court with the *Entrée* case. Visa and MasterCard quickly folded and abandoned their debit card merger, as described below. These events would eventually lead to the historic Merchants' case against Visa and MasterCard seven years later. The inside story of that second case, which lasted seven more years, is the subject of this book.

THE LAWSUIT FILED on October 25, 1996, is officially called *In re Visa Check/MasterMoney Antitrust Litigation.* It is sometimes referred to as *The Wal-Mart Case* or *The Merchants' Case against Visa/Master-Card* to distinguish it from a lawsuit brought by the United States against Visa and MasterCard two years later.

The Merchants' case and this book are about an effort to stop certain business practices and alter the anticompetitive structure of an industry using the U.S. antitrust laws as the instrument of change. That is what the antitrust laws were designed to do, and, once in a generation, what they actually achieve. In the Merchants' case, my law firm, Constantine & Partners, which had eight lawyers when the case began and 17 when it ended, represented Wal-Mart, Sears Roebuck, Circuit City, The Limited, Safeway, and a class of five million stores against Visa and MasterCard. These bankcard associations were joint ventures owned by most of the country's banks. Visa and MasterCard were represented by four of the largest law firms, including Clifford Chance, the biggest law firm in the world.

In *Means of Ascent*, Robert Caro quotes Lyndon Johnson as saying, "If you do everything you will win." I thought of that quote constantly throughout the case, and it became a mantra for our litigation team. But unlike Johnson, we didn't cheat. We did everything else and won.

The case was settled on April 30, 2003, after a jury had been impaneled for trial. Although the cash payment made by Visa and MasterCard to my clients was only the third most significant part of the settlement, that payment alone exceeded the combined total paid in the previous eight largest federal antitrust class action settlements. I began writing this book on November 23, 2003. It was important for me to begin writing then, because the court's award of attorneys' fees had not yet been made. Although many people involved, as well as most observers of the case, consider our fee to be the most interesting event, I consider it incidental. It is a collateral benefit or damage of the case, depending on the point of view.

During my moment of celebrity following the settlement, I was profiled in the *New York Times*, which ran the headline, "He Won't Discuss Money, But He Now Accepts Visa," and the subheading, "Settlement $3 Billion, Taking on MasterCard, Priceless." The money that I wouldn't discuss was the amount of our attorneys' fee, which had not yet been awarded, but was months later. It was important for me to begin writing about the Merchants' case without that event intruding, although I could not escape the influence of its brooding imminence.

The court estimated that the settlement would save stores and shoppers upward of $87 billion in the first decade alone. However, the actual tally for just these quantifiable benefits will not be complete for many years, after many moves and countermoves are made by merchants, shoppers, Visa, MasterCard, banks, and competing payment networks such as American Express, Discover, STAR, PULSE and NYCE. As these moves are made and the savings are tallied, and other unforeseen benefits accrue, more articles or books about this case may be written by others. This is mine.

PART I

—

ORIGINS

Opening Statement

———

IT'S A FALLACY that lawyers who specialize in big-case business liti-gation are wannabe athletes. We are athletes, and to be successful we must have some of the physical attributes required in other great sports, including extraordinary stamina.

The training for my sport and epic contest in the Merchants' case began under my father, Connie Constantine, a track star at Curtis High School on Staten Island, a boxer in Tuscaloosa, Alabama, and a football star at Syracuse University, who briefly played in the NFL. I was schooled and coached first in New York City, where I was born, and later on Long Island at Herricks High School, where I wres-tled, played tennis and was a football star but of a magnitude many notches below my father. Until he died, in May 1966, at the end of my freshman year at Williams College, my father—and mother—never missed any of my games or matches—not even a Friday afternoon freshman football game in Middlebury, Vermont—a fourteen-hour roundtrip from our home in Manhasset. After my father died, I lost interest in football but went through the motions for several more seasons.

Meanwhile, I was following the path of a stereotypical late '60s student activist at Williams. I attempted to levitate the Pentagon and worked for the McCarthy Campaign in the '68 New Hampshire Democratic primary. I tried to gain some understanding of what my black friends at Williams were experiencing by becoming an exchange student at Howard University during the disastrous '68 spring semester, when both Dr. King and Bobby Kennedy were murdered. I was a protégé of Professor Frederic Schuman, a brilliant apostle of world government. And although I am Jewish, another major influence at Williams was Conrad van Ouwerkerk, a radical Dutch Jesuit whose ethical framework helped support my evolving commitment to advancing the greater good. After confiding these typical youthful yearnings to these two professors and one other, Professor James MacGregor Burns, I took the consensus advice and headed for law school, with the comforting thought that Gandhi had been a lawyer.

After Williams, I unhappily attended Columbia Law School, graduating in 1972. The unhappiness was my fault, not the law school's. Columbia Law wasn't Williams and wasn't supposed to be. It was more vocational than I had expected. Moreover, Columbia didn't afford me four to five hours a day of basketball, squash and tennis. I would have quit law school had it not been for an internship that I got in a Legal Services office in Queens, New York, during my second year.

Clients of Legal Services are poor people who are usually grateful to get any kind of lawyer, even a student masquerading as one, as I did during my second and third years at Columbia. I gave my clients all the skill I had, which at first wasn't much. They gave me a reason to stay in law school and a sport where I really could excel. In my legal pleadings and briefs, and in the courtroom, I became an athlete of my father's caliber. I became the person I wanted to be. I was brash, audacious, brave and sometimes reckless.

After graduating from Columbia, I stayed in Legal Services for eight more years, litigating a series of civil rights and constitutional cases involving welfare and immigration statutes, abused prisoners and discrimination against the disabled, gay people and immigrants. I reveled in my role as an angry young man "speaking truth to power" for my poor and disenfranchised clients. But the real truth was that, although I cared deeply about my clients and "left it all out on the field" for them, I was working on my moves, using their problems as my training vehicle.

One day, during my first year out of law school, I went to the state appellate court in Brooklyn to file an exotic, but technically permissible, constitutional challenge to a provision of New York's Civil Practice Law and Rules. Using this technicality, the New York Attorney General had indefinitely delayed, without due process of law, payment of a badly needed money judgment I had won against the state for one of my welfare clients. While I waited in the clerk's office for a judge to sign the order to show cause, which was the procedure to get my constitutional challenge before New York's Appellate Division, Second Department, the court's legendary clerk, Abe Selkin, appeared and asked to speak with me.

Selkin was an old curmudgeon, famous for his intellect, his tyrannical rule over a pool of law clerks and his intolerance for any practitioner who couldn't navigate the Appellate Division's endless and seemingly senseless rules. So, when he appeared to speak with me, I was ready for a whipping. Instead, he complemented me on the papers I had filed. He told me that my arguments wouldn't be successful, but said they were a great piece of work and he offered me a job. He asked me, "Why are you wasting your time working for *these people?*" I didn't have to ask him what he meant, and simply responded with an impression of the then popular comedian, Cliff Arquette, whose stage name was Charlie Weaver. In a booming voice that filled the courthouse, I bellowed, "These are *my people*." He shook his head and walked away, and so did I, and I never turned back.

I felt like I had found my home, and during the next eight years the conviction grew that I would stay with Legal Services for my entire career. However, during what turned out to be my last two years with Legal Services, I had two cases that resulted in my leaving the job I had thought was my life's work. Both cases were class actions, a device used to represent a large number of plaintiffs who are all making the same or very similar claims against the defendants.

The first case was called *Jones v. Califano*. I represented a class of thousands of aged, blind and disabled people suing the United States and New York State for using a bureaucratic technicality to deprive them of part of their public assistance. I had shown that this technicality violated the law. But each time I sued, the government would pay off my client, the individual named plaintiff necessary to maintain a class action, and thus "moot" the dispute and defeat the class action. So, I kept on filing class actions, and when Federal Judge Kevin Duffy once again denied my class motion and dismissed the case, after Ms. Jones was paid off, I appealed to the United States Court of Appeals for the Second Circuit. I argued that the government and courts were playing a cynical game on the backs of my elderly and disabled clients. In a somewhat novel decision, the Second Circuit agreed with me and thousands of poor people were finally paid their full subsistence benefits.

Toward the end of the *Jones* case, I represented another class, this one comprising all the gay prisoners in the Brooklyn House of Detention, who were suing New York State and New York City for being deprived of certain "privileges" given to straight prisoners. These privileges included access to the prison gym, chapel, library and "dayroom." The excuse for this discrimination was that the gay prisoners were being protected from the straight prisoners. After we sued, the government quickly folded and found ways to allow the gay prisoners to use these facilities, but four of my clients wanted to continue the suit and obtain money damages for their mistreatment. I and my co-counsel, Professor Stacy Caplow of Brooklyn Law School, told our clients that there was virtually no chance that they would be awarded damages by a typical Brooklyn jury. Our clients were black, gay, convicted felons. One was serving time for a homicide. After a weeklong trial, a jury of white ethnics, including Italians, Greeks and Jews, found for our clients and awarded them $10,000 each—a result that shocked everyone in court and led to a second-page story in the *New York Daily News*, written in a tone of outrage, and intentionally paired with story about former Miss America Anita Bryant's anti-gay campaign.

Someone was watching these two class actions. A staff led by activists had been brought in by the new liberal New York Attorney General Bob Abrams. Bob had succeeded a moderately conservative Republican, Louis Lefkowitz. Bob Hermann, a senior lawyer on Abrams's staff, took note of my victories against the attorney general's office in these two cases and asked me if I wanted to work in the Abrams administration. Initially, I dismissed the idea, telling Hermann that I wasn't going to help the state deprive people of their civil rights and welfare payments. But Hermann told me that Abrams had brought in a new team and a new agenda. He said that the AG's office would now be on the same side as Legal Services and other activist legal groups—most of the time. He said I could prosecute affirmative public interest cases rather than defend the government. I asked what the "affirmative" litigation bureaus were. He named consumer protection, civil rights, environmental protection, securities and antitrust and offered me several middle-managerial positions in these bureaus.

Still skeptical, I said I wouldn't leave my great job in Legal Services for a middle manager's position. I would accept a bureau chief's position or nothing. He said they had just replaced all the Lefkowitz bureau chiefs except in antitrust and observed that I had no credentials for that job. He was right. Although I had enrolled in an antitrust course at Columbia eight years before, I had actually shown up at precisely one class, reading the cases on my own. That was the totality of my relevant experience. That, and the fact that I slept every night with a former antitrust lawyer for the Federal Trade Commission (FTC), my wife, Jan.

I said I would take that antitrust job or nothing, and convinced Hermann to recommend my hiring to Abrams. My distant, but favorable, recollection of antitrust law involved decisions written by Supreme Court Justice William O. Douglas, the lion of the disenfranchised and oppressed. Justice Douglas's antitrust decisions read like his civil liberties opinions; they left me with the impression that antitrust was to economic freedom what civil rights and liberties were to social and political freedom. I wanted to test that impression and wanted to test my skills against my high-priced Columbia Law classmates whose meat and potatoes were defending big antitrust cases.

I was scheduled to interview with the Attorney General several weeks later. I purchased a new suit and cut my shoulder length hair for the big day. However, the day before the interview, it was "postponed" with the false explanation that Abrams had been called out of town. Years later, I found out that when Abrams had read my résumé, he had refused to interview me and upbraided his staff for sending a person with no experience to head the largest state antitrust office in the country.

After the "postponement" of my initial interview in the early spring of 1980, a young partner at White & Case accepted the job but backed out after his wife realized that the job paid $40,000 (less than half his private sector salary, but almost double mine in Brooklyn Legal Services). My interview with Abrams was rescheduled for a new date several months after the cancellation, with another false explanation to me. Although I didn't know the real story, I was suspicious and annoyed, especially about the haircut. This time, I went into the interview with long hair and with "an attitude."

When Abrams asked the obvious question about my lack of experience, I attacked. I told him I had done some research and that his antitrust office was doing little or nothing. I told him I was a good litigator, that litigation was litigation, and that I could master a new substantive area quickly. Set back on his heels and somewhat amused, Abrams hired me. Or so I thought. Years later, he admitted that he had hired me because of my knowledge of New York Yankees trivia, revealed during the interview.

My initial ignorance of antitrust law was a great asset. I didn't understand all the things we weren't supposed to do, and I didn't understand the tertiary role of state antitrust offices, well behind the federal antitrust agencies and the private bar. Although antitrust law had once been primarily the province of state attorneys general, by the second decade of the twentieth century, antitrust law was dominated by massive battles among U.S. antitrust agencies and big private law firms. This relegated the states to the occasional small local dispute.

I brought to my new job the fervor and self-righteousness of a "poverty lawyer." I knew that my new causes and clients were right. Their goals of economic and market freedom were closely related to those of my former clients fighting for their civil rights and liberties. My new role as head of Antitrust Enforcement for New York State felt very much like my old job, and I started to rebuild my new shop on the model of a Legal Services office, hiring my old colleagues.

During the next eight years, as the Reagan administration abandoned, to all effects, antitrust enforcement and tried to repeal the laws through legislation and court advocacy, we took over. I began a movement in the antitrust offices of the state attorneys general. The AGs adopted uniform enforcement guidelines, which I wrote, that made it possible to collectively enforce the antitrust laws in cases and investigations involving groups of states. I was lead counsel in many of these. In the late 1980s, most of the difficult, visionary and cutting-edge antitrust cases emanated from the states. My student intern, Eliot Spitzer, witnessed these early efforts and got his first taste of how the states could flex their muscles and supplant federal agencies that were asleep at the switch. In some of these cases, five or ten states would band together. In one case, 19 states, in others, more than 40.

On my last day on the job, January 7, 1991, I filed and settled a case where, for the first time, all 50 state attorneys general joined together in a single antitrust case and sued Mitsubishi for fixing the price of video equipment. And the year prior to that, I led the 14 states that had sued Visa and MasterCard for merging their debit card operations as described in the opening of this book. That 1989 lawsuit, now referred to in the industry as the "*Entrée* case," forced Visa and MasterCard to abandon their joint debit card operation and laid the groundwork for the Merchants' case. The Merchants' case was the contest that I had been training for all my life.

The Cartel Revealed

THE PLAN TO boycott American Express was recklessly broadcast in a telegram sent on March 11, 1987, to 5,500 U.S. banks by Visa's CEO, Charles Russell. Russell warned the banks, members of both Visa and MasterCard, that American Express had just entered the credit card market with a revolving credit card called Optima. Russell's telegram, sent from Visa's sprawling, campus-like headquarters in the San Francisco Bay area, urged the banks to boycott American Express, to stop selling Amex Travelers Cheques and to terminate other business relationships with Amex.

Lawyers for American Express sent me a copy of the Visa telegram. Two things startled me: the blatancy of its call for a boycott of American Express and the explicit address to MasterCard banks as well as Visa banks. I soon learned that Visa and MasterCard were not really competitors. Visa and MasterCard then were, and still are, card networks and brands that also process electronic payment transactions. The same *big* banks—such as Citibank, Bank of America, Wachovia, Wells Fargo and Chase—called the shots at both credit card companies. These big bank owner/members of both companies offered virtually identical products. Some of these products were labeled Visa, and others MasterCard, but other than the paint job, the products were the same.

In what I learned was called Visa and MasterCard "duality," these same big banks ran Visa and MasterCard under virtually identical rules specifying the way that cardholders, stores and banks use their cards and networks. In fact, the networks held regular meetings to align these rules. This noncompetitive and anticompetitive system of duality was also bank jargon for the fact that virtually every bank that offered Visa credit cards to its customers also offered Master-Card credit cards on the exact same terms and price. Every store that accepted Visa credit accepted MasterCard credit. The two products functioned identically and were priced almost identically, despite the different names and advertising attempting to convey the impression that they were different.

Under duality, it made sense that Visa's CEO would explicitly call on "MasterCard" banks to boycott American Express. It made sense, but doing it so publicly was stupid. To an antitrust enforcer, it was like a front-page ad in the *Wall Street Journal* saying, "Just in case you were wondering, Visa and MasterCard don't really compete." That, precisely, was my interpretation of the Russell telegram.

Within days, I got the backing of most state attorneys general to threaten Visa and the banks with antitrust action unless the incipient boycott was called off. Within weeks, the banks that were in the process of terminating business relationships with American Express backed down, and the few who had already stopped selling Amex products rescinded their actions. Barry Brett, one of the outside counsel for Visa, described the Russell telegram to me as "an orphan with nobody willing to admit authorship."

Although the venality, misrepresentation and smugness of these companies was no worse than other industries I took on (with cable television springing to mind), Visa and MasterCard had something that set them apart for me. It was the sheer audacity of the cartel that they jointly coordinated: It comprised virtually every U.S. bank. Economics taught that cartels—organizations in which companies that would otherwise compete agree to fix and coordinate their prices and the products they offer—are unstable and that the greater the number of participants, the greater the instability. Visa and MasterCard allowed thousands of banks to act together: to fix prices, to promote inferior standardized products and to suppress competitors and competing technologies.

Initially, one group of big banks ran Visa, and another Master-Card. After duality, the same banks owned and ran both, allowing this massive cartel to operate and remain stable. The fact that this grand conspiracy was unconcealed and that neither the Department of Justice, the Federal Reserve, nor anyone else seemed to care, told me that this was my chance at improving something that affected every American.

Entrée: The Cartel's Assault on the Cashless Society

Our brief investigation of the boycott also disclosed that Visa and MasterCard had agreed to join forces in an emerging market by forming a new debit card network called Entrée. In explaining the competitive significance of this action to my staff and the state AGs, the best analogy I could come up with was a hypothetical merger of Coke and Pepsi to monopolize a new beverage market, one that would be much bigger than cola. The problem with that analogy was that Coke's and Pepsi's cola products really competed, while in 1987 Visa's and MasterCard's credit card products in reality did not.

By 1987, it was already clear to many people that debit card transactions would eventually far surpass credit cards. Predictions made throughout the 1970s and 1980s of the coming "cashless society" were shorthand for expectations of an enormous debit card market. By 1987, the explosive growth in the credit card market had begun to slow down. Despite the fact that most consumers had one or more credit cards and most merchants accepted them, more than 90 percent of retail purchases were still paid for with cash and checks. Almost all utility, mortgage, rent, insurance and other recurring payments were made with checks. It was foreseeable that most of these paper transactions would eventually be replaced by safer, faster and more convenient electronic debit transactions. So, the fact that Visa and MasterCard were barely competing in the credit card market was less important to me than their efforts to merge their debit card operations under the banner of the new Entrée debit network.

In 1987, there were more than a hundred regional and local ATM networks operating in the United States. Many, such as PULSE, STAR, Most, NYCE, Honor, Avail, Cactus, Accel and Yankee 24, had already, or would soon, become debit card networks by allowing their ATM cards to be used at stores with a personal identification number, or PIN, to purchase goods.

My office, joined by a dozen other state AGs, began an investigation of Entrée. We issued investigative subpoenae to Visa and MasterCard under the authority of New York's antitrust law and got the networks to agree that the information they produced could be shown to any other attorney general's office that wanted to see it. Throughout the 1980s, AGs used such multi-state antitrust investigations as a way of pooling scarce resources and collectively acting as a de facto national antitrust agency, without benefit of any statutory authority to do so.

Companies like Visa and MasterCard usually complied with the states' sharing procedure because, if they didn't, they could be forced to produce documents under separate subpoenae issued by twenty, thirty or even all fifty states. For years, because states actually did little antitrust enforcement, the possibility of facing so many state probes (a legal possibility throughout the twentieth century) was only theoretical. After a series of well-publicized efforts, in the 1980s, companies decided that it was better to submit to a coordinated multi-state investigation than to battle numerous separate state inquiries. So, in the case of Entrée, Visa and MasterCard seemed to submit passively.

But what I initially perceived as passivity by Visa and MasterCard was actually a blend of arrogance and condescension toward the states. That became clear as meetings with our adversaries became frequent. The bank associations were implicitly saying, "We're not afraid of you." They were going to teach us about the wonderful things Visa and MasterCard and their member banks had done for the world. They told us that they were the most efficient organizations ever conceived and that we would come to believe this just like our more important counterparts at the Reagan FTC and Antitrust Division. I had obtained portions of the Department of Justice's antitrust file on Visa/MasterCard under a law that made this confidential material available to state AGs. The file showed that the Antitrust Division knew what Visa and MasterCard were doing, and it demonstrated the federal government's tacit approval.

Visa was relying not just on the Department of Justice's laissez-faire attitude, but, in particular, on the *Nabanco* antitrust case in which Visa defeated a price-fixing claim made by a processor of its credit card transactions. Nabanco and other processors install terminals at checkout counters and route payment transactions to networks like Visa, MasterCard, Discover, American Express, STAR and NYCE for the network's permission to accept the card ("authorization") and for transferring funds to the merchant as payment ("settlement"). In 1979, Nabanco challenged Visa's practice of fixing the price of a fee that was paid by every merchant in every Visa credit card transaction. (Though the suit charged only Visa, MasterCard had the same practice of fixing the fee.) This fixed fee—paid to the bank by the processor, which then passes the charge along to the store—is called the "interchange fee." Regardless of the store, the processor, the merchant's bank, or the shopper's bank, this interchange fee was set by Visa. Nabanco claimed this was price-fixing, a basic antitrust violation. Nabanco also claimed that fixing these prices eliminated competition that otherwise would have occurred in the credit card market, with thousands of banks negotiating with hundreds of processors and millions of stores over the prices of accepting Visa credit card transactions. The artificially high prices for the credit transactions were raising the prices paid by the stores and their shoppers by hundreds of millions of dollars annually.

After five years of litigation, Visa prevailed in the *Nabanco* case. The U.S. District Court in Florida and the U.S. Court of Appeals for the Eleventh Circuit found that although Visa was fixing prices, an antitrust sin of the first magnitude, this particular price-fixing was not only benign but also a necessity for the Visa network to survive. The court lauded Visa for the imaginative way in which it formed a payment system among competing banks, as contrasted with the American Express and Diners Club systems, which were each owned by a single financial institution. The court said that this acceptable form of price-fixing couldn't harm competition in the credit card market, because there was no such market. The court opined that credit cards competed with cash, checks, money orders, travelers checks and debit cards in one big payment market, which the industry called the "Wampum" market.

Battles over market definition are often the most crucial contests in antitrust cases. The plaintiff defines the market narrowly. The defendant tries to broaden it. So, when the NFL was charged with monopolizing the professional football market, as it often was by competitors like the old AFL and USFL, it would respond (and has responded in many cases) that it competes with Major League

Baseball, the NBA, the WNBA, the NHL and even the Professional Bowlers Association for the hearts and minds of sedentary people. In *Nabanco*, the endorsement of the Wampum market was tantamount to a court not merely accepting the NFL's claim that it competes with professional bowling but also with movies, TV, radio, live theater and all other forms of entertainment. Visa and MasterCard waved around *Nabanco* like a cross at those who would dare attack them.

The State Attorneys General Terminate Entrée

Thirteen state attorneys general sued Visa and MasterCard on July 26, 1989. Utah joined later. The states' complaint alleged that Visa and MasterCard jointly monopolized the credit card market and that they were jointly attempting to monopolize the emerging market for debit card transactions. The complaint detailed MasterCard's previous acquisition of the Cirrus national ATM network, Visa's previous acquisition of the Plus national ATM network, and Visa's control of the Interlink debit card network. We alleged that, under the banner of the new Entrée network, Visa and MasterCard intended to monopolize and control the development of the debit card market.

Prior to the complaint, Visa and MasterCard had already eliminated their most important competition by buying or controlling the Cirrus, Plus and Interlink networks. When Visa and MasterCard acquired Plus and Cirrus, they knew that these national ATM networks were planning to make their ATM cards function at stores as debit cards, using the cardholder's same PIN. Visa and MasterCard prevented Plus and Cirrus from doing that and becoming integrated ATM/debit networks. Limited to ATMs, these networks were uniquely inefficient. They were like telephone companies whose lines couldn't be used for Internet access.

Visa's cooption of Interlink was the flip side of what MasterCard and Visa did to Cirrus and Plus. Interlink was a debit-only network, and by far the biggest. Interlink had more than half of all the PIN-authorized debit transactions in the United States. Visa bought control of Interlink and never allowed the system to become an ATM network. Years later, Visa took other actions to suppress Interlink and use it as a baseball bat to clobber the regional ATM/debit networks such as STAR, NYCE and PULSE. But I am getting ahead of the story.

In July 1989, all that we knew was that Visa and MasterCard had already picked off the three most important competitors in the debit card market: Cirrus, Plus and Interlink. In the *Entrée* complaint, the combination of these four debit mergers, (1) Visa with MasterCard in Entrée, (2) MasterCard with Cirrus, (3) Visa with Plus and (4) Visa with Interlink, were collectively alleged to be an attempt and conspiracy to monopolize the debit card market. These are violations of Section 2 of the Sherman Antitrust Act, the basic federal antitrust law passed in 1890, called the "Magna Carta" of free enterprise by the United States Supreme Court. We also alleged that these mergers violated Section 7 of the Clayton Act, the anti-merger provision of the federal antitrust laws.

The *Entrée* complaint explained how these mergers would not only stifle competition in the future but were already doing so. In a harbinger of the Merchants' case that I would file seven years later, the 1989 complaint explained that Visa and MasterCard each had a debit network operating over its credit card system with transactions authorized by signature instead of a PIN. It asserted that these so-called "off-line" debit transactions were much slower, much less secure and much more expensive for stores than so-called "online" PIN debit transactions. The complaint also alleged that most stores incorrectly believed that these off-line signature debit card transactions were credit card transactions.

Visa and MasterCard and their banks charged merchants the same price for signature debit card transactions as for credit card transactions—without the loan provided in a credit transaction, and with only a tiny portion of the risk. The complaint asserted that the Visa and MasterCard debit cards looked exactly like their credit cards and that this design choice was intended to fool stores so they wouldn't get mad about paying high-risk credit card prices for low-risk debit card transactions.

The stores that did know about these signature debit cards paid these high prices because they were coerced by so-called "tying arrangements," that force a person to buy a group of products, in order to get the one desired product. When Microsoft says, "If you want my operating system, you have to buy my web browser, or my media player," that is tying. Under the guise of Visa's and Master-Card's virtually identical "Honor All Cards" rules, any store that accepted Visa and MasterCard credit cards was forced to accept their debit card transactions at the same price as credit.

The complaint explained how the Visa/MasterCard joint debit venture would extend beyond the Entrée network into the transaction-processing business, where Visa and MasterCard maintained separate systems. If Entrée was not stopped, these competing systems would eventually be connected, and one of the few remaining ways that Visa and MasterCard competed would be eliminated.

The complaint explained the regrettable history and effects of duality. Duality, also called the "virtual" or "creeping" merger of Visa and MasterCard, was prohibited in other parts of the world. In Canada and Europe, banks had to choose either Visa or MasterCard in order to maintain competition. In the rest of the world, there was no joint Visa/MasterCard debit network under any name. Visa and MasterCard, which were born and bred and had well over half of their business in the U.S., didn't compete here but did everywhere else, with a predictable result: better products and lower prices everywhere but home.

The *Entrée* complaint was filed in July 1989. The judge assigned to the case was Pierre Leval, ironically a former partner of Terry Cone, one of the witnesses to MasterCard's expensive dinner at Rusty Staub's. The complaint had several goals and faced several obstacles. The basic objective was to terminate Entrée and lay the basis for a debit card market with much more competition than existed in the credit card market. A broader goal was to undercut duality and begin to force MasterCard and Visa to compete.

The major obstacles to these objectives were bad legal precedents and bad antitrust policy and enforcement by the federal antitrust agencies. The worst of many bad legal precedents was *Nabanco*. If Judge Leval were to adopt the overly broad wampum market definition like the judge in the *Nabanco* case had, we would lose. We would not be able to show that Visa/MasterCard seriously threatened to dominate a payment market that included cash and check transactions, whose dollar value then far exceeded the comparable numbers for credit and debit cards combined.

Another obstacle that not only hampered the states, but to some extent created the competitive problems we were trying to fix, emanated from errors made by the United States Department of Justice in 1975. In that year, the Antitrust Division helped to create the competitive abomination of Visa/MasterCard duality. During their formative years, Visa and MasterCard actually competed. Visa had a rule that prohibited a bank from simultaneously issuing Visa credit cards and MasterCard credit cards. This rule resulted not only in competition between the two credit card associations but also in competition between Visa banks and MasterCard banks. The Worthen Bank from Arkansas, which wanted to issue both brands of cards and wanted to own a piece of both associations, helped eliminate that competition.

It challenged Visa's anti-duality rule under the antitrust laws. Visa won an important appellate court decision in the *Worthen* case and appeared headed for total vindication. However, Visa went to the Antitrust Division seeking support and approval of its anti-duality rule and was turned down. The Antitrust Division didn't condemn the rule outright but wondered out loud whether prohibiting banks from joining and owning a piece of both associations harmed competition.

At least one state helped the federal Antitrust Division create this competitive nightmare. Arkansas filed a "friend of court" brief supporting Worthen. The brief was written by a young University of Arkansas law professor named Bill Clinton, who soon would become Arkansas' Attorney General. Clinton's legal brief in support of Worthen's anticompetitive position was apparently the beginning of a long and mutually beneficial relationship between the lawyer and the bank. Later highlights included a crucial loan to the Clinton gubernatorial campaign in 1990 that was orchestrated by Worthen owners at a time when the governor's re-election was in jeopardy; a $2 million loan in 1992 to his presidential campaign, funding a media blitz to counter the Gennifer Flowers revelations; a 1994 fire in Worthen headquarters, where some Whitewater documents were stored; and persistent allegations that Worthen received special treatment during Clinton's terms as governor.

The Antitrust Division's position was more important than Arkansas' support for Worthen. Lacking any government backing, Visa repealed its anti-duality rule. In the next few years, every large bank and most medium-sized banks in the United States became owner/members of both associations and issued both brands of credit cards. The fact that the Department of Justice was principally to blame for this problem was not lost on anybody, least of all Visa. Visa capitalized on the elimination of MasterCard as a competitor and gleefully pointed out that the Antitrust Division had "made us do it."

Visa used this argument as a defense in many antitrust cases and government investigations. The tactic worked well at the federal agency level, where the lawyers seemed to be traumatized by the doctrinal sins of their predecessors. An investigative file given to the States by the Reagan Antitrust Division discussed the "creeping merger" of Visa and MasterCard but concluded that the Division would not do anything about this until there were an actual merger. While the associations crept closer together, the federal agencies slept. They acquiesced in the Plus and Cirrus acquisitions, and when an "actual" merger came along in the form of Entrée, the federal agencies again did nothing. This federal laxity gave the states and me our opening.

During the *Entrée* pre-complaint negotiations with the associations, Visa and MasterCard tried the "U.S. made us do it" defense on me, but only half-heartedly. It was common knowledge that the states, under my direction, had set themselves up as a de facto national agency to fill the void left by federal non-enforcement of the antitrust laws. At the time, business periodicals reported frequently on this clash of "antitrust federalism." In fact, on March 11, 1987, the day that the infamous Russell telegram was sent to the 5,500 Visa and MasterCard banks, I was flying back from Washington with Bob Abrams and reading the *Wall Street Journal's* coverage of an "in your face" action we had spearheaded the day before, when the States had adopted the "Horizontal Merger Guidelines" I had written. The *Journal* reported:

> "In an unusual attack on the Reagan administration's antitrust-enforcement policies, the National Association of Attorneys General unanimously adopted merger guidelines intended to slow the pace of major corporate takeovers. The move, announced

by a bipartisan group of eight attorneys general representing every region of the country, indicates the extent of state opposition to the administration's generally hands-off approach to merger enforcement. It also sets the stage for a more aggressive and better coordinated effort by States to challenge merger proposals in Court."

Bob Abrams's attention, first riveted to our major story, was soon destroyed by his discovery that Phylicia Rashad was sitting right in front of us. I then ended any attempt to discuss with Bob our next move in the states-versus-feds antitrust wars.

My colleagues and I laughed during the July 1989 meetings when Visa and MasterCard told us that the federal agencies had encouraged duality and had acquiesced in the formation of Entrée. But after we filed the *Entrée* complaint, we were concerned that "the federal government made us do it" defense might work with Judge Leval, who had earned his spurs at Cleary Gottlieb, a big firm whose mainstay was defending large antitrust cases.

Another obstacle to the success of our case was the fact that all of the mergers—Visa, MasterCard, Cirrus, Plus and Interlink—attacked in the *Entrée* complaint had been consummated before we went to court. In 1989, the U.S. Supreme Court had not yet decided whether a state attorney general could get a federal court to require the breakup of a completed merger, even if the AG could prove that the merger had been illegal and was causing harm to the marketplace. The remedy of a breakup or divestiture was only clearly available to the federal antitrust agencies back then, and those agencies wanted to keep that divestiture remedy exclusively to themselves. They weren't challenging very many of the enormous corporate mergers of the 1980s, and that neglect, from which our economy still suffers today, was intentional. It created many of the "too big to fail" companies that taxpayers are now being forced to bail out.

The federal agencies didn't want anyone else to enforce the anti-merger law either and had gone to court to narrow the scope of private enforcement of these laws. They had even gone to Congress unsuccessfully seeking what effectively would have been repeal of Clayton Act Section 7, the anti-merger provision of the antitrust laws. Directly to the point, on the day we filed the complaint seeking the disintegration of *Entrée*, the United States government was in the Supreme Court trying to block the California Attorney General from getting a group of stores divested from the Lucky and American Stores supermarket chains, which had merged illegally.

We also faced widespread judicial hostility to undoing completed merger transactions. Courts simply didn't (and still don't) like to require a breakup after a deal has closed. They refer to it as "unscrambling eggs." This reluctance gets stronger the more time passes. The courts ask, "Where were you when this was all happening? Why didn't you stop it before it got to this point?" And the answer to those questions has to be very compelling to have any chance of success. In 1989, my potential answers were not persuasive. My most candid answer would have been that "when this was happening, we weren't thinking about Visa and MasterCard and naively relying on the federal agencies to enforce the antitrust laws."

The most important thing we had figured out in our investigation was that Entrée was designed as much to retard the development of the debit card market as to make Visa/MasterCard the dominant force in a rapidly expanding business. Although expansion of the debit market was inevitable, the pace of expansion could be slowed by a monopolist. Visa and MasterCard wanted to suppress PIN debit when they formed Entrée. The banks feared that PIN debit transactions would replace many lucrative credit card transactions, especially where a plastic card was being used merely for convenience and not to obtain credit. The banks understood that PIN debit was faster, safer and cheaper than their signature debit card systems and, if allowed to grow, would quickly put the Visa/MasterCard signature debit card programs out of business.

The banks also viewed those hundred-or-so little ATM/debit networks around the country, like NYCE, MAC, STAR and Shazam, as not only debit card competitors that had to be stopped, but competitors who might expand and, in the future, challenge their lucrative credit card monopoly. These ATM/debit card networks already had banks issuing their cards, consumers carrying them and merchants accepting them. They had card-processing facilities. All they had to do was expand from local to regional to national networks and then enter the credit card market. Their credit cards could be then authorized by a PIN rather than a signature, which was safer, faster and more efficient. While Visa/MasterCard and their banks had lots of reasons to retard the growth of debit and to dominate that business once it became big, their most important objective was to protect Visa/MasterCard's credit card monopoly. The overarching allegation in the *Entrée* complaint was that the new network was not really designed to operate actively so much as serve as an obstacle to the expansion of other fledgling debit card networks.

Entrée fell apart as soon as we filed the complaint. Visa and MasterCard beat their breasts and made noises about fighting until vindicated. In truth, this was just posturing, and the associations' lack of resolve soon became apparent. I believe one reason they quickly threw in the towel was MasterCard's post-traumatic stress, resulting from our discovery of their discussion about threatening me. Bob Norton, the MasterCard general counsel, absented himself from meetings and court appearances. MasterCard didn't seem to want to litigate against me, presumably because of their fear that I would use the

Rusty Staub's incident against them at some crucial juncture in the litigation.

A second reason had to do with the sibling rivalry that had developed between Visa and MasterCard because of duality, a rivalry that was further exposed by the Entrée merger. Each sibling was constantly trying to show their bank parents that they were the smarter kid, and each believed that the other was holding her back. The result was numerous disputes about seemingly trivial issues. One such dispute involved a fight about whether an Entrée debit card could also display the Visa or MasterCard logo. Visa wanted its proud and handsome logo on the cards. MasterCard, somewhat hysterically, predicted that putting Visa's or its own nondescript MasterCard logo on a card that also had the Entrée brand would set in motion a sequence of events that ultimately would destroy the lucrative Visa/MasterCard card networks. A consultant, Booz Allen Hamilton, was hired to arbitrate this dispute, ultimately deciding in favor of Visa's point of view. This unleashed a torrent of recrimination by MasterCard against both Booz Allen and Visa, the likes of which had not been heard since Regan was ragging on sister Goneril to King Lear. Killing Entrée would momentarily separate the siblings and give each the opportunity to show the banks which network could develop the debit card market more profitably. For fans of the TV show *Dallas*, think of J.R. and Bobby Ewing vying for Jock's affection by showing who could make more money for "Ewing Oil."

A third reason Visa and MasterCard folded so soon after the Entrée complaint was their desire to limit their loss to Entrée, instead of also jeopardizing the previously completed acquisitions of Cirrus and Plus and the imminent consummation of Visa's purchase of Interlink. Another likely reason for Visa/MasterCard's spiritless and quickly abandoned defense of Entrée was their fear of what the states would uncover if full pretrial discovery were to go forward. Lots of very nasty stuff from the 1980s was produced a decade later during the pretrial exchange of documents and depositions in the Merchants' case. All of that and much more would have come to light a decade earlier had the *Entrée* case gone forward.

With little fanfare, and before a single document was produced, or a single deposition taken or any motions filed by either side, the defendants told me that they would abandon Entrée if our case would go away. In a series of meetings held separately with Visa and MasterCard, though no longer attended by the hibernating Master-Card General Counsel Bob Norton, we negotiated the *Entrée* consent decree, which was signed on May 8, 1990. The *Entrée* decree also required Visa and MasterCard to give the state attorneys general expedited notice and disclosure of various actions, which raised competitive red flags—such as Visa/MasterCard joint activities and acquisitions of competing debit, credit, or ATM systems.

At a credit card industry conference in Denver, Colorado, on October 4, 1990, three days after the death of *Entrée,* I took a victory lap and delivered a requiem for the network. I also spoke about other antitrust issues facing the payment systems industry. I told the audience of bankers, merchants and payment network executives that the *Entrée* case was just the beginning of a series of antitrust cases that would confront the plastic card industry during the decade.

Going Private

A FTER ENTRÉE WAS terminated, I decided to leave the New York Attorney General's office. I had been there for more than a decade, and it was time to move on. For one thing, the State antitrust movement and our quest for recognition as a "national" agency was becoming a cult of personality—mine. The focus on me was symbolized by MasterCard's crude and naïve assumption that threatening me would make the states go away. It also trivialized and devalued the work of scores of talented people in state attorneys general offices around the country. I could feel the resentment of colleagues welling up and wanted to leave while things were still friendly.

At the same time, the pull of new cases was making it difficult for me to leave. By mid-1990, my office was spearheading a 44-state investigation of a joint venture in which the largest U.S. cable TV systems, including Time Warner, TCI, Cox, Comcast and Continental, had joined forces with General Electric in the "K-Prime," later called "PrimeStar," Direct Broadcast Satellite ("DBS") system. Our theory about PrimeStar was similar to our claims about Entrée. We claimed that this satellite venture was an attempt by cable television monopolists to slow the pace of a competing technology (DBS) and monopolize the new satellite technology when it finally developed.

My office was also leading multi-state investigations of alleged price-fixing by Mitsubishi and Nintendo, the third and fourth of our multi-state price-fixing cases against Japanese consumer electronics conglomerates in three years. We had successfully sued Panasonic and Minolta the previous two years. Years later, I would get the attention of my antitrust students at Fordham Law School by reading aloud from Michael Crichton's *The Rising Sun*, where a character refers to four of my cases and says:

> "Yeah. And we're looking at Nakamoto. My sources keep telling me Nakamoto's going to get hit with a price-fixing suit. Price-fixing is the name of the game for Japanese companies. I pulled a list of who's settled lawsuits. Nintendo in 1991, price-fixing games. Mitsubishi that year, price-fixing TVs. Panasonic in 1989. Minolta in 1987. And you know, that's just the tip of the iceberg."

But back in 1990, I realized that if I were to defer my departure until my new cases were over, other cases would just replace them, and I would either never leave, or more likely be kicked out by a new attorney general who would replace Bob Abrams. It was clear by mid-1990 that Bob would run for the Senate in 1992 against Al D'Amato, who was engulfed in a series of scandals that left him vulnerable. So, I started looking for a job while trying to get as much done as possible. Before I left, we sued Mitsubishi. This was the first time in which all 50 states joined to bring an antitrust case. We settled this case on my last day with the New York Attorney General's Office, January 7, 1991.

On January 8, 1991, I became a partner in the New York office of the large, Chicago-based law firm McDermott Will & Emery. That first day, Andy Somers, the General Counsel of American Express, had lunch with me and asked me to represent American Express in an antitrust dispute with Visa. He said he had followed the *Entrée* case closely and had waited until I left government to hire me. I was ecstatic. When you enter private practice from government, you have no business. You go from being in demand to being the new boy with no clients, nothing to do and no power within your firm. Your impotence continues until you get your own business. And three hours after arriving at McDermott, I thought I had the type of client and business that would give me instant credibility. It also promised to keep me involved in payments systems antitrust—a specialty that I egotistically believed "belonged to me."

I never got to represent American Express, because my firm never permitted it. When Amex called, I did a "conflicts check" designed to make sure my work for them would not conflict with the firm's work for other existing clients. The conflicts check came back clean. But in a large firm like McDermott, every partner gets to see the conflicts check and to consider the proposed representation. They consider whether, in addition to an actual conflict, there may be an "issue conflict" putting the firm on the side of an issue that another client might not like. Other partners in the firm may even consider whether they want the new guy to take on a case that might make it harder for them to get some new business in the future. Those "aspirational conflicts" stopped me from representing American Express.

Three weeks later, Visa hired me to represent them in an antitrust case against Discover. When Visa retained me, I thought it was natural and logical. I was an antitrust star. I knew the industry. As Bennet Katz, Visa's General Counsel at the time, said, "You have just knocked our brains out—I want you on our side, and I think you will agree with Visa on this issue."

Visa had just been sued in an antitrust case by the Discover credit card network, then owned by Sears Roebuck. A Sears subsidiary had just bought a little bankrupt industrial bank in Utah called the Mountainwest Industrial Loan Corporation. Mountainwest was a member of Visa (and MasterCard, of course) and had issued a few thousand Visa credit cards. Using this little bank, Discover planned to issue millions of Visa credit cards as part of a plan to eventually shift cardholders to Discover, in part by offering them more favorable terms. This would greatly expand the Discover network. Discover's position, and the gist of its antitrust complaint against Visa, was that competition would be increased if it could issue Visa credit cards as well as Discover credit cards.

When Visa found out about Discover's plan, it ordered the company licensed to manufacture Visa credit cards to stop the presses. But in trying to stop Discover from becoming a member of Visa, I thought Visa was probably right from the standpoint of competition policy. Regardless of the evil in Visa's heart and its numerous antitrust sins, especially against Discover and American Express, I viewed a world in which Discover and American Express became members of Visa/MasterCard as a competitive problem. So, I agreed to represent Visa on this narrow, but important, antitrust issue along with its usual antitrust firm, Heller Ehrman White and McAuliffe, based in San Francisco. The antitrust points were debatable, the economic theories involved were elegant and the case was likely to be fun.

Two hours after I agreed to represent Visa against Discover, a representative of Discover called to ask whether I would help represent Discover in the same case. I declined, explaining that I was already on the other side. In the next hour, I was invaded by self-doubt, not about my agreement to help Visa, but about whether I would have said yes to Discover if they had just called before Visa. Thinking about this was extremely uncomfortable for me at the time. I was still so thoroughly a public interest lawyer that the thought that I would simply agree to represent the first client who called was horrifying. Of course, this is what lawyers frequently do, and is their job to do. But at 43 I was still a virgin. The true answer to the uncomfortable question about Discover is unknown, like most "what ifs." But I think I would have represented Discover had they called first. The points in the dispute were close and debatable. Visa was an antitrust predator generally, if not in this specific instance. But most importantly, I needed the business and the interesting work.

For the next month, nastiness was directed at me on three fronts, eventually forcing me to withdraw from my representation of Visa. The first attack came from American Express, who went to my former boss, Attorney General Bob Abrams, complaining that there was something unethical about me representing Visa after so recently suing Visa. One doesn't have to know anything about legal ethics to understand how silly this charge was. Indeed, representing Discover against Visa soon after the *Entrée* case might have given Visa some cause for complaint, as they might have incorrectly inferred that confidential information obtained about Visa in my government capacity was being used against them in a private dispute. But the notion that the expertise attained by a government lawyer can't later be used by that lawyer in private practice, even in defense of a former opponent of the government, is unknown to the law unless government secrets are being used. Nevertheless, American Express went on a rampage calling as many of my former colleagues in the states as they could to register complaints against me.

My former colleagues also reacted angrily to my representation of Visa. They seemed ashamed that I was "selling out" just weeks after leaving my post as their leader. They may also have been releasing some pent-up hostility about all the press I had been getting for their efforts. I might have resisted all that, but my law firm ordered me to drop the case. A month after the new case had passed a conflicts check, it tardily came to light that one of the McDermott partners in Chicago was doing some tax work for Dean Witter—a corporate affiliate of Discover.

That was that, and it proved to be exceedingly lucky for me. In my unhappy month of representing Visa, I never examined a confidential Visa document, nor did much more than make one trip to Salt Lake City to watch a court argument, one trip to D.C. to talk to the staff at the Antitrust Division, and try to defend myself. Had I not been forced out so quickly, and stayed long enough to delve into confidential Visa documents, I might not have been able to later represent the merchants in their case against Visa and MasterCard. I became convinced that payment systems antitrust no longer had a place for me. American Express and Discover now hated me. Visa was annoyed that my firm had yanked me almost immediately after my agreeing to represent them. MasterCard? Not after the Rusty Staub's incident. No way for either side—never!

Later in 1991, a few months after the Visa/Discover fiasco, I got a call from Ralph Spurgin, the head of a private-label credit card business owned by The Limited, Leslie Wexner's specialty retail empire. Spurgin, an athletically built owner of Harleys and 12-cylinder cars, had heard me speak about the antitrust implications of various payment industry practices and wanted to discuss one of them. He flew to New York from Columbus, Ohio, and met with me and my law partner Larry Fox.

Spurgin, a tough guy, was angry about the tying arrangements that forced The Limited to accept Visa and MasterCard debit card transactions because they accepted Visa and MasterCard credit cards. He complained that the price of the debit transactions was the same as for credit cards, with no justification. He also complained that the debit cards were designed to look like credit cards. Spurgin had conducted a test with help from a bank in Minneapolis. The Limited found out how many of the Visa and MasterCard transactions that The Limited assumed were credit, were in fact debit card transactions. The test also showed that this small problem was steadily getting bigger. Spurgin complained that these signature debit transactions, which cost The Limited roughly $1.50 for a $100 purchase, were displacing cash and check transactions that cost The Limited only a dime or less. The Limited couldn't say "no" to these transactions, nor could they even figure out when they were getting these disguised debit cards, except by getting their bank to do an "after the fact" test.

Spurgin hired me to do an analysis of a potential lawsuit against MasterCard. He and I believed that MasterCard was the weaker of the two associations. It had a much smaller signature debit program and was actively promoting a PIN debit program, and for these reasons MasterCard was more likely to fold if sued than Visa. Larry Fox and I did the analysis, which concluded that The Limited had viable antitrust claims against MasterCard.

After reviewing our analysis, Spurgin wanted to file suit. The Limited's Chief Financial Officer, Ken Gilman, sent threatening letters to both MasterCard and Visa. He demanded that the associations stop forcing The Limited and its sister stores, Victoria's Secret, Abercrombie & Fitch, Lane Bryant, Lerner, Bath and Body Works and Bendels, to accept signature debit transactions and demanded some mechanism for his stores to be able to distinguish the debit cards from the credit cards so they could be rejected.

Visa and MasterCard both responded that they could, and would, continue to force these stores to take their debit card transactions. Because Visa and MasterCard credit cards were the primary credit line of most U.S. shoppers, The Limited really had no choice. Spurgin and Gilman wanted to sue. But Leslie Wexner, The Limited's CEO and principal owner, had reservations. He knew that a lawsuit against Visa and MasterCard was effectively a suit against virtually every U.S. bank. He had a strong relationship with Banc One of Ohio, then one of the biggest Visa/MasterCard banks.

Furthermore, Wexner didn't have much use for lawyers. At the time, his company had $8 billion dollars in annual sales but did not have a single lawyer on its payroll. There was nothing personal in this, as Leslie later married a lovely lawyer from the New York law firm of Davis Polk and quickly had a bunch of cute kids. One of these, an adorable little girl, climbed all over him years later while I was trying to prepare him to be deposed by Visa and MasterCard. Wexner's real aversion was not to lawyers, but litigation. He saw it as a wasteful diversion from The Limited's mission to sell clothing and be the premiere specialty retailer in the world.

In 1991, Wexner couldn't see the justification for a big and expensive lawsuit to stop a practice that was only costing The Limited a few hundred thousand dollars in excess charges each year. When he was told that the problem would get bigger, Wexner said that when that happened, then maybe he would sue. More importantly, he asked why, if this was such a big problem, The Limited was the only store willing to stick its neck out by suing the banks. Gilman and Spurgin told me to keep the potential case on my radar screen and that they would keep it on theirs. They would track the increase in forced signature debit card transactions, and I would update the antitrust analysis as the facts and law developed.

During the next four years, I frequently revised the analysis of the potential lawsuit. Moreover, from time to time, at The Limited's request, I sent the analysis to other large merchants. Each merchant that reviewed the analysis was convinced that the forced acceptance of signature debit card transactions was a growing problem, more than doubling each year. They all praised the analysis. However, each declined to join The Limited in suing Visa and MasterCard. With the exception of the *Entrée* case, well-known in the banking industry but little-noticed elsewhere, Visa and MasterCard had a perfect record in fending off antitrust challenges.

The Founding of C&P

While this unsuccessful mating dance with potential litigants against Visa and MasterCard was going on, I decided to leave McDermott Will & Emery and open an antitrust boutique with some friends from various placed I had worked during my career. These included Carol Turner from McDermott as well as several associates from that firm; Bob Begleiter, a guy my age, who, like me, was an ex-Legal Services lawyer; Jeff Shinder, a young Canadian lawyer; Abby Milstein, a consumer protection lawyer; and Eliot Spitzer.

Eliot and I had known each other at that point for a dozen years. In the summer of 1982, the third year of my decade running New York State's antitrust office, Eliot, an intern from Harvard Law School, came to work for me in the South Tower of the World Trade Center. Before we met, Eliot's résumé put me slightly on guard because of my bad experience the previous summer with a similarly configured intern. The 1981 version had been from Yale Law School and, like Eliot, was a member of the law review. The Yalie was a rich kid of famous parentage who had come to work with the attitude that my job was to provide him with a fun summer.

After Eliot strode into my office in June 1982, he needed only five minutes to dispel my preconceptions. We quickly exchanged names, schools, favorite sports and pedigrees, but his subtext was "I am smarter than you, and I can beat you at tennis, squash, skiing and any other game you want to play." My subtext was "Good luck—give it your best shot." Almost three decades later, that unresolved contest continues.

We were kindred spirits, similarly motivated by a desire to use the law to make things better. But in 1982, I could already see that Eliot had advantages I lacked, which destined him for high elective office. He had youth. He had been president of the student body at Princeton—a good sign that he desired public office. Unlike me, Eliot had money. And, as I did, Eliot loved constitutional law. However, he, more than I, believed in the power of government to help people. In 1982, I was still a skeptical outsider relatively new to government. In fact, I was still technically on a "leave of absence" from Legal Services—a psychological security blanket I did not surrender until 1984.

Eliot and I understood our similarities and our differences. I had spent the summer after my first undistinguished year at Columbia Law as a hardhat working on the Manhattan construction site of One New York Plaza, near Battery Park in Manhattan. Eliot spent his summer after election to the Harvard Law Review in my state antitrust office. But we shared similar world views, and with the mutual realization that we each had found an ultracompetitive "other" to bump chests with, it was respect and admiration at first sight.

After spending the summer of 1982 principally working on a criminal antitrust prosecution of ambulance companies who had divided the Syracuse region into little monopolies where they would not compete, Eliot returned to Harvard. We stayed in touch, and after Eliot graduated and completed a clerkship for United States District Judge Bob Sweet, I advised him to go directly into government in a prosecutorial role. It took no exceptional analytical skill to see that Eliot would be a great prosecutor. Instead of taking my advice, Eliot went to Paul Weiss, then perhaps the most cerebral of New York law firms. But tardily realizing the wisdom in my advice, Eliot left Paul Weiss in less than a year to join Bob Morgenthau's staff in the Manhattan District Attorney's office.

Eliot quickly rose to head Morgenthau's labor racketeering bureau, and in that role I deputized him to act as a special assistant attorney general so that he could utilize New York's antitrust law in a prosecution targeting the Gambino crime family's control of garment center trucking. The attorney general jealously guarded this prosecutorial tool, and I had denied other district attorneys' requests for permission to prosecute criminal antitrust cases. But Bob Abrams and I considered Eliot to be one of our own.

In the early 1990s, Eliot and I both moved to big firms: he to Skadden Arps, and I to McDermott Will & Emery. Neither of us was satisfied. I was conflicted out of representing the big companies that tried to hire me to represent them in plaintiffs' antitrust cases. These included American Express, General Electric, Dean Witter and, ironically, Visa, among others. Eliot was merely treading water until his opening to run for elective office.

In early 1994, we commiserated and made a plan. I would leave McDermott to form an antitrust boutique, and he would leave Skadden and enter the Democratic primary for Attorney General. I did not expect that Eliot would win. The goal, at least in my view, was to establish his visibility, laying the groundwork for Eliot's second and real run for statewide office. I proposed that he join my soon-to-be-established firm and promised him that our firm would give him all the room and time he needed to make that expected second run for elective office.

The plan worked perfectly for everybody. Eliot did much better than expected in the 1994 Democratic primary. He did not win, but he got over 20 percent of the votes in a four-way race and earned the endorsement of both the *New York Daily News* and Rupert Murdoch's *New York Post*. Eliot joined us as one of the "name" and "founding" partners of Constantine & Partners (C&P) during the first few months of our existence. For the next three and one-half years, Eliot billed about 2,000 hours annually, good years for most lawyers, but about half the time Eliot actually worked during that period. The balance of his time was spent laying the foundation for his next and successful run for New York Attorney General. At the firm, Eliot took a major role in representing Liberty Cable, did some antitrust work for Rupert Murdoch, and most enjoyably represented William "Kid Chocolate" Guthrie, a "contenda" for the World Light Heavyweight Boxing Championship. Guthrie had been deprived of a shot at the title because of alleged restraints of trade involving boxing promoter Don King. When C&P won Guthrie's antitrust case, the kid got his shot, knocked out the champ and thanked Eliot and the firm from the ring on national TV.

The October 1996 complaint in the Merchants' case lists Eliot as one of the five lawyers representing the plaintiffs. The fee petition I filed seven years later details Eliot's one and one-half billed hours. Eliot actually billed another hour, but I "wrote it off" along with thousands of other hours when I prepared the attorneys' fee petition. Eliot frequently tells me that his were the crucial 90 minutes in the case.

Constantine & Partners, the firm Eliot, Carol, Bob, Abby, I and the others had started to build in 1994, had its genesis in a conversation between me and Howard Milstein, the husband of Abby Milstein, one of the other founding partners. Howard claimed that Time Warner was trying to destroy Liberty Cable, a "wireless" cable company that, using microwave technology, competed with Time Warner in New York City. Liberty, which delivered superior service at a lower price, had started to make serious inroads into Time Warner's New York City cable monopoly until blocked by what Milstein claimed was a variety of predatory practices.

Howard Milstein, like my partner, Abby, was a Harvard Law graduate. He also had an economics degree from Cornell, *summa cum laude*, and held a Harvard MBA. He was a billionaire and a tenacious competitor. Howard convinced me to start C&P so that he could have the lawyer and champion he wanted and a law firm conceived and dedicated to winning his big antitrust case.

In early 1994, there was a final meeting to discuss the pros and cons of starting the firm. The attendees were Abby, Howard, me and my wife Jan, who was then the General Counsel of Rupert Murdoch's News America Marketing and Publishing. Jan had been an antitrust lawyer at the Federal Trade Commission years before I entered the antitrust field. She is an experienced trial practitioner and deal lawyer and was there to protect me and our family.

When the financial side of forming C&P was acceptable to Jan, we all shook hands and kissed, and Howard said that C&P would be the perfect firm to win his perfect antitrust case against Time Warner. I told Howard that his case was good, but I cautioned that it would be a very tough case against very tough opposition—Time Warner and their excellent antitrust counsel, Cravath, Swaine & Moore. I also predicted that Leslie Wexner and The Limited would eventually become clients of our new antitrust boutique and that C&P would file and win an even tougher case, one that I considered to be the "perfect antitrust case," the one that would become the Merchants' case.

In 1995, a year after C&P opened, The Limited got back in touch with me, this time through their very first lawyer and General Counsel, Sam Fried. As promised, The Limited and I had kept the problem of signature debit on our respective radar screens and tracked its rapid expansion. Leslie Wexner was now convinced that The Limited should sue Visa and MasterCard. However, Wexner still wanted at least one other merchant to join him in the lawsuit.

In November 1995, right after the Veterans Day weekend, I got a call from Steve Hunter, Wal-Mart's payment guru, who had received my antitrust analysis from The Limited. Hunter is the epitome of what has made Wal-Mart so successful. He is a big, smart, no-nonsense country boy, who abandoned luxury and high compensation at GE Capital for Arkansas and the Spartan conditions and equity stake that Wal-Mart offers its employees. Hunter agreed with my analysis, and he wanted to retain C&P and consider joining The Limited in a suit against Visa and MasterCard. I had been working toward this day for years and had a draft complaint almost ready to file. However, it was nearly a year until we filed the Merchants' case on October 25, 1996. During that year, C&P began to learn what it would be like to represent Wal-Mart.

Wal-Mart,
The Double-Edged Sword

———

Now with the active litigation over, I can see how important Wal-Mart was to the effort. It was at once our biggest asset and biggest challenge. Representing them was frequently a pleasure and honor but often as difficult as opposing Visa and MasterCard and, at times, more difficult, painful and frustrating. All of that is clear now, but at the beginning I saw neither how important Wal-Mart would be, nor how difficult. I really didn't see it as being any more important than the other big merchants I represented. That had to do more with my ignorance and Manhattan tunnel vision than with reality.

As of November 1995, when Steve Hunter, Wal-Mart's payment director, contacted me after reading the antitrust analyses I had written for The Limited, I had never been to a Wal-Mart store. There weren't any in Manhattan (or, indeed, anywhere in New York City), where I was born, raised my three children and will call home until I die. Eliot and his wife, Silda, were fans of Wal-Mart, buying all the stuff for one of C&P's summer outings at the Wal-Mart in Kingston, New York. So, I finally went to a Wal-Mart in 1998, two years after we filed the Merchants' case, and then only because I thought it prudent to visit the stores of each of our clients and personally inspect the checkout areas where they accepted payment. When I finally got there, I quickly realized what all the applause and boos were about.

I don't need to describe what a Wal-Mart looks like, how low the prices are, or the appearance and demeanor of its sales associates. Most of my readers will know, and knew about this before me. However, my experiences during that first visit to a Wal-Mart stayed with me. One thing that favorably impressed me was the large number of variously disabled workers. The second was the palpable devotion of Wal-Mart shoppers.

While there, my wife Jan and I bought an upright vacuum cleaner and a folding table with four chairs. At first, we couldn't select a vacuum cleaner, because they were all so inexpensive that despite the name brands, we doubted their quality. Another shopper, sensing our confusion, literally took us by the hands, helped us find a very good machine, and delivered an unsolicited, but heartfelt, commercial for Wal-Mart. She told us that Wal-Mart allowed her family to live a better life and have better things in their home than they ever had before. She said her daughter had asthma, but that with the excellent Eureka vacuum that she had purchased at Wal-Mart (and persuaded us to buy), her daughter's attacks were less severe. We found the folding table on our own, the kind that stores four chairs inside and folds up and rolls on its own wheels. Two decades before, we had purchased a similar table from Hammacher Schlemmer for $500. It was a nice, serviceable piece, made with wood veneers, and had fallen apart after many years of use. Twenty years later, at Wal-Mart, we were buying a better, sturdier, solid-wood version for $120. Everything else about Wal-Mart is as simple and as complicated as that.

The low retail prices are not merely the product of the low prices that Wal-Mart pays its suppliers and the low wages it pays its employees. Wal-Mart systematically eliminates excess costs from every step in the distribution chain. They are not hypocrites, unlike so many other companies I have encountered. They walk the walk. Rob Walton, Sam Walton's son, and Wal-Mart's chairman, works in a small, windowless office. When I started visiting Wal-Mart's home office in Bentonville, Arkansas, in 1997, the entire corporate headquarters contained only one conference room, called the "Quail Room," proudly displaying Mr. Sam's hunting photos.

Low wages are paid to Wal-Mart executives and lawyers, as well as to Wal-Mart sales associates, but Wal-Mart stock and options are widely distributed to employees at every level. Employee equity, which has created loyalty and devotion to Wal-Mart and to its customers, is widespread and palpable. You can't buy a Wal-Mart executive a meal or a drink or send her a Christmas present. After our holiday gifts were politely returned, C&P switched to making donations in honor of all our clients and friends to charities such as City Harvest and Meals on Wheels. Wal-Mart employees, generous and polite themselves, will afford you every courtesy and give you the shirts off their backs.

Wal-Mart's obsession with cost-cutting works well, except in discrete situations such as the purchase of lawyers' services. Wal-Mart thinks that hiring outside counsel is like buying tube socks. It's not, and Wal-Mart has paid dearly while learning that lesson, having been sanctioned in numerous courts for discovery abuses, such as failing to turn over relevant documents and evidence. I don't know whether those claims about Wal-Mart "hiding the ball" in other litigation were true or not. In our case, Visa charged that Wal-Mart had destroyed relevant evidence. C&P's experience successfully defending against that claim—which, had it been successful, might have derailed our case—showed no venality or bad intent on Wal-Mart's part. It did show rampant cost-cutting in litigation expenses—a realm where the platitude "penny wise, pound foolish" usually fits.

Wal-Mart came to me in 1995 because they realized that though they paid less for everything else than any other merchant, they paid exactly the same high prices for Visa and MasterCard services. And like every other store, they were forced to take Visa and MasterCard debit card transactions at credit card prices. When Wal-Mart politely asked Visa's CEO, Carl Pascarella, to stop forcing it to accept these debit card transactions, Pascarella bluntly responded that Visa could force it to. And right after that impolite retort, Wal-Mart hired me and C&P.

Preparing Wal-Mart and The Limited for Battle

Wal-Mart was the best possible plaintiff and class representative for this case but also the most difficult client I have ever represented. But the extraordinary difficulty of the case was one of the things that made it the perfect antitrust case. Dealing with the big egos of all my clients, their various litigation objectives, and the diverse corporate cultures at each huge company was as or more difficult than any other part of the case. So, the year of getting Wal-Mart into the gate was good practice for what was to come.

Part of that year (November 1995 to late October 1996) was spent trying to get a government antitrust agency to file its own case. Wal-Mart required that we make this effort. I really didn't want this to happen, because I wanted to control the case. I thought a government agency would interfere with our case and/or screw up its own. However, it was my job to make the effort to get an agency involved, and so I tried.

I met with Joel Klein, who was Deputy Assistant Attorney General and later would become the head of the federal Antitrust Division. Joel and I were like a pair of Siamese Fighting Fish, two tough Jewish kids from the same lower-middle-class Queens neighborhood, who clashed every time we met. We would each say that we fought because we disagreed, but the real reason was our similarities.

I also met with numerous state attorney general antitrust chiefs. All of these meetings were cordial, but the implicit and sometimes explicit response was that Wal-Mart had the resources to bring its own antitrust case. The fact that Visa's and MasterCard's practices hurt millions of small merchants and virtually every U.S. consumer, did not seem to resonate with my former colleagues.

I also made an effort to interest the Federal Trade Commission in this cause, as the FTC shares the federal government's antitrust jurisdiction with the Department of Justice. I met with Christine Varney, an FTC Commissioner; Bill Baer, the FTC's Competition Bureau Director; and FTC Chairman, Bob Pitofsky. Pitofsky said that our facts were interesting but that there really wasn't any tying arrangement involved in Visa/MasterCard's practices. He said that even though stores were forced to accept signature debit card transactions, they were still free to accept other forms of payment as well. This pronouncement, which contained a basic legal error, confirmed to me that getting the government involved in our cause would be of little help, and might actually hurt. Pitofsky, a renowned antitrust scholar, a personal hero, and, in my estimation, the best federal antitrust enforcement official of the last thirty years, remembered that early 1996 meeting. Seven years later, after we won summary judgment on the tying claim, which asserted that stores accepting Visa/MasterCard credit were forced to accept their debit transactions,. Pitofsky went out of his way to admit his skepticism and to congratulate me for staying the course. Pitofsky's admission was doubly gracious, given the fact that after he left the FTC in 2001, he joined Arnold & Porter (A&P), one of the two firms that represented Visa in the Merchants' case.

Although Wal-Mart had come to me, it was clear that they

weren't quite sure what they were doing with me. C&P was new, small, and virtually unknown to them. Wal-Mart had gotten a positive reference about our firm from lawyers at the New York law firm, Weil, Gotshal & Manges, but this recommendation helped only so much. C&P was not only an unknown quantity to Wal-Mart, but the role of the injured antitrust plaintiff, a reversal of Wal-Mart's usual defendant status, made the potential lawsuit, and their leading role in it, seem strange to them. The corporate culture of Wal-Mart identified with defense arguments and the defense bar. On top of this, the case had to be filed as a class action. This was almost too much to bear for a company constantly fending off class actions.

I explained to Wal-Mart and The Limited that once they filed an antitrust case, there would be copycat class actions filed by other antitrust firms representing nominal clients. Unless we preemptively filed the case as a class action—the other firms would turn it into a class action and seize control of the litigation. Wal-Mart would be at the mercy of firms like Milberg Weiss and Hagens Berman. Wal-Mart despised such firms because they believed that plaintiffs' lawyers were constantly filing frivolous class actions against Wal-Mart. Wal-Mart eventually accepted the fact that our case had to be filed as a class action, but that fact continued to rankle them on principle.

Months of discussion about the fee arrangement then ensued. Wal-Mart was famous for buying everything—including the services of lawyers—cheaper than anyone else. When my friends at Weil Gotshal called to tell me that they had sung my praises to Wal-Mart, they implicitly warned me to be careful for what I wished for. They said that Wal-Mart would relentlessly force me to lower fees and swallow costs. Armed with this knowledge, I counterpunched as soon as Wal-Mart demanded fees lower than our normal billing rates. Our rates were low for New York, but higher than Wal-Mart was accustomed to paying firms based in Fayetteville and Little Rock, Arkansas.

I told Wal-Mart I would take the case on a contingency fee basis—meaning that they would pay no legal fees unless they recovered damages. Our fee would come from their recovery, if any. I believed that the idea of being a class representative in a big contingency fee class action was so alien to Wal-Mart that they really didn't know what to do, but say yes. I informed The Limited that since Wal-Mart would go the contingency fee route, they should as well, and they agreed.

Seven years later, an attorney representing one of the class members objecting to our attorneys' fee application told the judge:

"What Class Counsel did here seems to be to be a little bit crazy. They risked the firm. It was a bet the firm case on a case that really seemed to be a negative lawsuit. It really looked like a huge longshot."

When it became clear in 1996 that no government antitrust agency would file its own case, I was authorized by Wal-Mart and The Limited to finalize a complaint. We went through 14 drafts, including one several hundred pages long with an extensive set of annotations detailing the proof supporting each allegation. Many lawyers consider a complaint something like a lob serve in volleyball. They don't use it as a weapon but merely as a device to get the game going. The conventional view is that the complaint should be a short and simple document setting forth just enough facts to meet the requirement of putting the defendants on notice about the nature of the legal claims being made against them. I use a different type of complaint, a "singing complaint," which exhaustively details the facts and tells a story. A complaint like this gives the judge an immediate education. It gives reporters something to write their stories with and contrasts favorably with the typically opaque and formulaic "deny, deny, deny" mantra in defendants' answers.

In the Merchants' case, there would be extensive press coverage. The names of the parties alone would be newsworthy. The fact that corporate giants were suing, instead of being sued, in a class action, was "man bites dog" offbeat. The issues were important but hard to explain. We needed to explain them to a class of millions of U.S. stores that we purported to represent. We would never be able to directly communicate with even a small fraction of these stores. The best we could do was to allow the story to be told simply and clearly in the press and to create court documents that reporters could easily use to write their own stories.

The complaint was going to be the first of these court documents. In the 13th and penultimate draft complaint, like the first 12, Wal-Mart and The Limited sued Visa and MasterCard in a purported class action on behalf of every merchant in the U.S. that accepted Visa and MasterCard credit cards. The complaint called the plaintiffs "merchants," a term more expansive than "stores" or "retailers." Merchants included entities such as colleges, charities and government agencies that also accept plastic cards for payment.

The 14th version of the complaint, which was filed in the United States District Court for the Eastern District of New York in Brooklyn on October 25, 1996, named Visa as the only defendant. The complaint plainly said that MasterCard was equally culpable for the antitrust violations alleged, but treated MasterCard as an unsued, but named, coconspirator.

At the last minute, Wal-Mart asked that MasterCard be given a chance "to do the right thing." To its credit, Wal-Mart, the most frequently sued business in the world, really didn't like litigation. Its conservative and Southern world view considered litigation a breakdown in polite business dealings. The people at Wal-Mart are genuinely polite, from Rob Walton, Wal-Mart's Chairman, to the cashiers whom Wal-Mart gracefully calls "sales associates." These associates make up almost 1 percent of the U.S. workforce. In 1996, Wal-Mart had just allowed the Chase Bank to issue a MasterCard credit card cobranded with the Wal-Mart name. Wal-Mart had received a lot of money for allowing its name to be used by Chase and MasterCard in this way. It didn't seem right to Wal-Mart to take that money and then quickly turn around and sue MasterCard on an unrelated antitrust claim, not without giving them the chance to do the right thing. Wal-Mart was sure that when MasterCard was asked politely by its biggest customer, it would stop forcing Wal-Mart to accept unwanted MasterCard signature debit cards. Wal-Mart's Steve Hunter had previously made the same request of Visa. Visa's CEO, Carl Pascarella, had responded by saying that Visa could force Wal-Mart to accept the unwanted signature debit cards. Wal-Mart thought MasterCard would be different. I knew better. MasterCard would not back off, even at the request of Wal-Mart. MasterCard had earlier responded to a similar request by The Limited with a condescending refusal couched in almost identical terms to Visa's refusal. Moreover, it would have been a very good move for MasterCard to grant Wal-Mart's request. That is why Visa wouldn't permit MasterCard to do it.

I knew that Visa had more than four times as many signature debit card transactions as MasterCard. MasterCard had tried, years before, to emphasize the much safer, much faster and much less expensive PIN debit technology using a new network it had formed, called Maestro. The tying arrangements that forced merchants to take Visa and MasterCard signature debit and suppressed PIN debit helped Visa much more than MasterCard. Most rational businesses in MasterCard's position would have granted Wal-Mart's request, realizing that it would force Visa to match this position or risk a massive defection of stores. But because of duality, MasterCard couldn't possibly say "yes" to a strategy that would benefit MasterCard but hurt Visa.

The merchants' October 25, 1996, complaint against Visa was purportedly filed not just for Wal-Mart and The Limited, but on behalf of millions of stores. It explained the history and facts of duality and began to teach the court, the press and the unwitting merchant victims how Visa/MasterCard fronted for a U.S. bank cartel. The complaint alleged that thousands of banks were coconspirators. They owned both Visa and MasterCard and forced merchants to accept both brands of debit card transactions with contracts that included identical tying arrangements. The largest of these banks, such as Citibank, Bank of America and Wells Fargo, called the shots in both associations.

Although banks didn't simultaneously sit on the boards of both Visa and MasterCard, it was common for a bank on the Visa board to serve on a governing body of MasterCard or vice versa. A good example of this was Norwest Bank, which served on the Visa board while at the same time serving on MasterCard's so-called Business Committee, a group with significant clout within the MasterCard association. Banks also hopped right out of one bed and into the other, like Citibank, which went directly from the Visa board to the MasterCard board. Flaunting these facts before the federal Antitrust Division, MasterCard's General Counsel, Bob Norton, had asked the Department of Justice to exempt MasterCard and Visa from the law that bars simultaneous service on the boards of two competing businesses. In his letter seeking an exemption from the law concerning such "interlocking directorates," Norton argued that MasterCard and Visa "simply do not compete in any conventional business sense."

You don't have to be an antitrust expert to realize how foolish it was to say this to the Antitrust Division. For sheer stupidity, it was the MasterCard analog of Visa's CEO sending a boycott telegram to

5,500 banks and invoking their membership in MasterCard. Norton made this request in a letter to the Department of Justice in 1992, three years after the events at Rusty Staub's. Norton sent a copy of his letter to his outside antitrust counsel, Stanley Robinson, at the Kaye Scholer law firm. That was three years after Robinson's law partner had told me that Stanley was about to retire as part of his plea that I not press ethical charges against Robinson or Kaye Scholer.

The merchants' complaint also explained how almost identical exclusionary rules adopted by Visa and MasterCard kept American Express and Discover from entering the debit card market, and how these rules also marginalized the Discover and American Express credit card businesses. Echoing Bob Norton's statement to the Antitrust Division, these exclusionary rules blatantly proclaimed that Visa and MasterCard were not competitors. They shouted this by exempting each other from rules designed to block the expansion of competing payment card businesses.

In May 1991, for example, Visa had adopted By-law 2.10(e), a rule that barred its banks, meaning virtually every bank in the U.S., from issuing an American Express or Discover brand credit or debit card or the cards of any other network that Visa considered to be a competitor. Visa said that its banks could issue MasterCard credit cards, meaning that Visa didn't consider MasterCard a competitor. Visa didn't allow banks that issued Visa branded debit cards to also issue MasterCard branded debit cards because of the injunction terminating my earlier case involving the Entrée debit card network. Visa's enactment of By-law 2.10(e) finally got the Antitrust Division off the dime, 19 years after the division had acted as the midwife for "duality." In 1994, the division began an investigation focused on Visa's exclusionary and inflammatory by-law.

MasterCard could have enjoyed this moment. Visa, not Master-Card, was under government scrutiny. MasterCard got the full benefit of the Visa rule without lifting a finger. Because virtually every Visa bank was also a MasterCard member, the Visa rule effectively prohibited MasterCard's banks from issuing an American Express, Discover, or any other competitive card. However, MasterCard emulated Visa and stuck its neck out with nothing to gain and everything to lose. MasterCard passed a rule virtually identical to Visa's, which MasterCard called the "Competitive Programs Policy," or CPP. The CPP, like Visa's rule, targeted competitors, but as Visa had exempted MasterCard, Visa was also exempt from MasterCard's policy. Both companies were brazenly screaming, "We don't consider each other competitors."

On March 27, 1997, I had lunch with Joel Klein, by then the head of the Antitrust Division. Klein was meeting with progressive antitrust experts to solicit ideas for his newly won stewardship of the division. We discussed the recently filed Merchants' case and the investigation of the Visa/MasterCard exclusionary rules that he had inherited from his predecessor, Anne Bingaman. I pointed out the irrationality of MasterCard's passage of the CPP. I explained that this was an example of MasterCard showing the banks that it would throw itself on the railroad tracks next to Visa in a public demonstration of anticompetitive solidarity. I said it was also a show of confidence that his Antitrust Division would do nothing about it. Boys are boys. Despite the fact that Klein and I were pushing 50, we were both kids from Queens, each tough in our own way, and I was throwing down a dare.

Klein said he was convinced, and soon after our lunch, an investigation widely viewed as going nowhere started to pick up steam. M. J. Moltenbrey, the attorney supervising the Antitrust Division's investigation of Visa and MasterCard, invited me down to Washington, D.C., to pick my brain. This was the first in a series of such meetings where C&P tried to educate the division's lawyers to think about

Visa/MasterCard in the way we did and to overcome the agency's two-decade inertia borne of its 1975 duality mistake.

Nineteen months after my lunch with Joel Klein, and two years after we filed our complaint, the United States sued Visa and MasterCard over their system of duality and also over their exclusionary rules that targeted American Express and Discover. The focus of the United States' case was the credit card market. The Merchants' case had focused on the debit card market and showed how Visa/MasterCard not only blocked Discover and American Express from that market using their exclusionary rules, but also retarded the growth of other competing networks and the competing online PIN debit technology.

A basic article of faith in antitrust is that a better and less costly product will marginalize, if not completely eliminate, an inferior and more expensive product. In a competitive market, the superior product will win quickly. However, this clearly was not a competitive market. As our October 1996 complaint detailed, the comparison between Visa/MasterCard signature debit and PIN debit was qualitatively and quantitatively one-sided.

Signature debit cost merchants roughly $1.50 per $100 transaction, compared to roughly 7¢ for PIN debit. Signature debit transactions were also seven to ten times more likely to be fraudulent due to the ease of forging a signature. Stores had virtually stopped trying to teach modestly educated sales clerks to even attempt to verify that the signatures on payment cards and sales slips matched. Documents that were later obtained in discovery showed that Visa knew that an attempt to verify a cardholder's signature occurred only eight percent of the time.

A signature debit card transaction also took two to three times longer to complete at the checkout counter than a PIN debit transaction. Signature debit took two to five days to transfer money from a shopper's bank account to the store's account. In PIN transactions, this transfer between accounts took less than a day, and a hold was placed on the money in the shopper's account at the time of the purchase. This hold prevented shoppers from inadvertently spending the same money several times and/or spending money they didn't have. By contrast, the delayed and uncertain clearance time for signature debit transactions caused a significant increase in bounced checks. Banks liked this because they collected fees of $25 or more from both shoppers and merchants for every bounced check. Only the banks—and Visa and MasterCard—benefited. PIN debit was not only much faster, safer and cheaper, but also superior to signature debit in virtually every way.

Our October 1996 complaint explained why stores faced with this disparity between signature and PIN debit on price, safety and speed didn't and couldn't "just say no" to Visa and MasterCard signature debit. Visa and MasterCard debit was tied to their credit card transactions. Stores couldn't stop accepting Visa/MasterCard credit, because doing this would eliminate the stores' ability to access the primary credit account of virtually every U.S. shopper. By 1996, there were very few stores that didn't accept Visa and MasterCard credit cards. The complaint alleged that once such a holdout store started to accept Visa/MasterCard credit, there was no turning back. That allegation, made on instinct and personal observation, proved true. In the hundreds of depositions of Visa/MasterCard executives and experts that followed in the coming years, not one could name a single store that started to accept Visa or MasterCard and then stopped. And not one executive could name a single store that accepted Visa credit cards but not MasterCard credit cards, or vice versa. The merchants' inability to say "no" explained why despite the fact that PIN debit was far superior in all these ways, Visa/MasterCard signature debit had more than twice the market share of the more than 50 competing PIN debit networks. Indeed, signature debit's market share was increasing, despite its qualitative inferiority and much higher price.

The complaint also alleged that identical tying arrangements between Visa/MasterCard credit transactions and signature debit transactions were at the core of the competitive problem. The tying arrangements forced merchants to take an unwanted product. These tying arrangements, which Visa and MasterCard called their *Honor All Cards Rules,* made it less likely that the PIN debit networks would expand to challenge Visa/MasterCard in the lucrative credit card market. The merchants' complaint also explained two additional predatory tools used by Visa/MasterCard. One was a massive campaign to prevent merchants from being able to tell the difference between a credit card and a debit card, and the second the defendants' anti-steering rules.

When we filed the complaint, we knew that most merchants had no idea they were even accepting Visa/MasterCard signature debit transactions. The minority of stores that knew still could not distinguish debit cards from credit cards at the checkout counter. We were aware that the defendants had taken steps to deceive merchants, but we were not aware of the full extent of the deception. We also didn't know that the defendants understood that cardholders were also being badly confused, resulting in bounced checks and other consumer problems. The defendants did little to alleviate these problems because cardholder confusion was a necessary consequence of deceiving merchants about the identity of Visa/MasterCard debit cards. We found out about all this later, during the pretrial discovery process.

The rare merchant who figured out that it was getting a Visa/ MasterCard debit card transaction, instead of a credit card transaction, was barred under the defendants' "anti-steering" rules from taking any action to discourage the use of the debit card or encourage the shopper to pay with a different form of payment, such as PIN debit. These rules dictated that a store couldn't ask for another form of payment or surcharge the Visa/MasterCard debit transaction or even give a discount for an alternative form of payment, except to give a discount for cash. The rules were backed by the sanction of a store losing the "privilege" of accepting Visa and MasterCard credit cards.

When we sued in October 1996, these Visa/MasterCard anti-steering rules were absolutely clear on these points. However, after we sued, the defendants invented a defense, indeed their primary defense, based upon the supposed ability of stores to "steer" shoppers away from using Visa/MasterCard signature debit cards if the stores didn't want to accept signature debit transactions. The defendants said that if Miss Jones tried to pay for her lingerie at Victoria's Secret with a Visa or MasterCard debit card, the sales clerk could ask her to pay with a different card or a check or cash, and maybe give her a discount if she did. The defendants never denied that the stores had to take Visa/MasterCard debit transactions, but they claimed that the stores really wanted to take them. If they didn't, Visa/MasterCard argued, the stores would simply ask for a different form of payment or offer a discount for one, and most times that tactic would work.

As discussed, this type of steering was clearly prohibited by the defendants' rules. But after we sued, the defendants adopted elaborate cover stories claiming that these anti-steering rules didn't mean what they said and were never enforced. The defendants' steering defense, which involved a crude and obvious effort to change the facts, eventually became a bigger problem for Visa/MasterCard than the anti-steering rules themselves. The cover-up is usually worse than the "crime."

The forced displacement of safer, faster and much cheaper forms of payment had already cost merchants hundreds of millions of dollars, and those losses were escalating. In drafting the complaint, I first confronted an issue I believed would be a key jury problem in the trial expected to occur three years later (not nearly seven years as it turned out). Merchants who were forced to pay excess costs covered them by raising the prices charged to all shoppers. I believed this fact would be important to the jury, but I was uncertain which way it would cut. The jury would be mad at Visa/MasterCard because consumer prices had been unfairly and illegally raised by these tying arrangements. However, they might also conclude that if shoppers were the primary victims, it was unnecessary and even wrong to award a large monetary recovery to the merchants. Then again, a juror might argue, "If we don't award damages to the stores, Visa/MasterCard will get away with murder." Skillfully presenting this fact to a jury would be very difficult.

Within weeks of filing, the case got the attention of other merchants and trade associations. Many stores called me and asked to join the case as named plaintiffs alongside Wal-Mart and The Limited, rather than continuing to be unnamed and passive class members. The named plaintiffs, also called "class representatives," get to exercise significant influence and control over the litigation. We said yes to those who we thought would help the case by adding weight, commitment and good facts.

C&P agreed to represent Sears, then the largest department store; Circuit City, then the largest consumer electronics chain; and Safeway, then the nation's second largest supermarket. I knew that Safeway understood the issues as well as or better than any store in the country. In the five-year period between The Limited hiring me and the filing of the complaint, Safeway had approached me and indicated their awareness and concern about these issues and some inclination to sue. However, instead of suing Visa, Safeway had brokered a deal with Visa for lower credit card rates for themselves and all supermarkets. That deal had proven a disaster. Even at the lower supermarket credit card rates, much cheaper cash and check transactions were replaced by Visa/MasterCard credit and debit transactions. Moreover, people didn't buy more broccoli just because they could use a credit card. Safeway and the other supermarkets were locked in, and they couldn't stop accepting Visa and MasterCard credit cards after making this Faustian deal. Safeway came into the case sadder and wiser.

All of the many stores that asked me to allow them to join Wal-Mart and The Limited in the caption had similar motivations—the potential for achieving lower debit card rates and freedom from Visa/MasterCard coercion. Sears and Circuit City also had their own special reasons. Sears was a major player in the credit card industry, having created the Discover network and sold it profitably. It also owned the massive Sears credit card business, which was then more profitable to Sears than the sale of merchandise. Sears also hated Visa, because it believed that Visa had tried to destroy Discover from the moment it went into business. Circuit City had a General Counsel named Steve Cannon, who formerly was chief counsel of the U.S. Senate's Antitrust Subcommittee, chaired by his boss, Senator Strom Thurmond. Cannon also had been the No. 2 enforcement official in the Reagan Antitrust Division. He wanted a piece of a high-stakes antitrust case to spice up his steady diet of shopping mall leases, corporate work and cases where Circuit City was the defendant.

C&P took on these additional representations of Safeway, Sears and Circuit City but rejected several large store chains because we didn't like their motives for wanting to enter the case. Some of them seemed star-struck and anxious to join what they thought was a litigation dream team. Plaintiffs should enter litigation soberly and reluctantly. These volunteers reminded me of the joyous young confederate soldiers in an opening scene of *Gone With The Wind*.

We also rejected some strong and resolute stores, including Kroger, then the largest U.S. supermarket, since surpassed by Wal-

Mart. Kroger was a sober, serious and well-informed potential litigant. However, the case was getting unwieldy. C&P had only eight lawyers when the Merchants' case was filed. I realized that representing five of the largest merchants in the world, searching their documents, defending their executives at depositions and learning the intricacies of each of their companies would be difficult enough. Kroger did not provide anything to the case that Safeway hadn't already provided. Kroger was adamant and suggested that if C&P wouldn't represent them, they could find other counsel. I flew to Cincinnati, met with Kroger's CEO, general counsel, CFO and chief information officer (attended a Cincinnati Reds game with the GC) and spent two days successfully dissuading them from entering the case. I promised Kroger that because the Merchants' case was a class action, Kroger would be treated as well as the named plaintiffs. I told them they would actually be treated even better, because Kroger's documents wouldn't be searched, nor their executives deposed, nor would they encounter all the unpleasant and onerous obligations of a class representative carrying the banner of the entire retail industry.

Among the many other stores we rejected, one more is worth mentioning. Home Depot contacted me and said they wanted in. Later they said that it was politically unpalatable to be a plaintiff in a class action, even a "good one," because they hated class actions. They said they were a defendant in many class actions and most painfully in cases alleging various forms of employment discrimination. Therefore, they didn't want to do anything that might give aid and comfort to class actions. Though frequently sued for engaging in various forms of discrimination, they couldn't themselves "discriminate" between being a defendant and being a plaintiff or between a meritorious class action and a frivolous one. I thought it fortunate that they weren't entering the case. Almost seven years later, Home Depot's counsel called me and demanded that his client have a "seat at the table" in the settlement discussions, which they were sure would soon occur. They threatened to "opt out" of the class unless I acceded to this demand. I told them that the named plaintiffs, who had carried the case on their backs for seven years, had the only seats at the table alongside me. Home Depot opted out and pursued its own lawsuit against Visa and MasterCard, which was entirely based upon our work and legal victories. Their very big additional recovery came as the result of our efforts and the sacrifices made by our clients.

One common theme expressed by most of the stores that asked C&P to represent them as additional named plaintiffs was their concern that the giant stores that were class representatives would not adequately represent their interests. I assured them that this was not true. Making sure that the interests of every class member were given equal regard with those of Wal-Mart was my job. Nonetheless, I was also concerned about this issue of powerful clients and potential big-store bias. It was not so much concern for a conscious slant toward the interests of Sears, Wal-Mart and the other giants as concern about only hearing the views of the biggest players. No small store approached us, and we weren't about to solicit any. However, I was approached, and agreed to represent, three large retail trade associations, whose members included stores of all sizes.

The National Retail Federation (NRF), the International Mass Retail Association (IMRA) and the Food Marketing Institute (FMI), whose small and large store members had annual sales of over $1 trillion, asked to become plaintiffs. C&P gladly agreed to represent them without any fee, contingent or otherwise. I believed that these associations would be a constant source of industry expertise and would keep us honestly focused on the concerns of all stores.

I had some background with each of these trade associations. IMRA, later called The Retail Industry Leaders Association, had been a client of McDermott Will & Emery, the large law firm where

I had been a partner for three years. On several occasions, I had been a speaker on antitrust issues at meetings that FMI regularly held for the general counsel of U.S. supermarkets. I had also spoken at NRF's annual convention in early 1997. At that time, I told the CEOs of many of the largest retailers in the U.S. that they each were paying millions of dollars in excess charges, and because of Visa's and MasterCard's deception, they probably didn't even know it.

After our dream team of Wal-Mart, Sears, Circuit City, Safeway, The Limited, FMI, IMRA and NRF was in place, we added MasterCard to the case as a defendant. The seven plaintiffs other than Wal-Mart did not share Wal-Mart's opinion that MasterCard would do the right thing. Wal-Mart eventually found this out for itself, and MasterCard was sued as Visa's codefendant by all eight.

The Teams Line Up

———

IN THE WEEKS after the merchants' October 25, 1996, complaint was filed, the defendants assembled an army of lawyers to squash and humiliate C&P, the little firm that dared to wage war against the U.S. banking industry and its plastic card cartel. Visa retained two firms, its longstanding outside counsel, Heller Ehrman White & McAuliffe (HEWM), based in San Francisco and Washington-based Arnold & Porter (A&P).

Heller Ehrman and Visa, more than any other lawyer/client pair I have encountered, were mirror images. They were smart, slick, self-assured and quintessentially California. And the truth is, I liked and respected both. In contrast to San Francisco-based HEWM, A&P was thoroughly Eastern, D.C. establishment and a firm with unique stature in antitrust for many reasons, including its namesake Thurman Arnold, a famous head of the federal Antitrust Division from 1938 to 1943.

To say that Visa retained Heller Ehrman conveys the misimpression that there was a process of deliberation and decision resulting in this representation. That didn't happen. Heller Ehrman had been antitrust counsel to Visa for decades. The functioning and structure of Visa are products of antitrust counseling and litigation done by

Heller Ehrman. Visa and MasterCard were each joint ventures of virtually all U.S. banks. These banks were supposed to be competitors. Because of this, Visa and MasterCard were constantly subject to antitrust scrutiny and attack. So, the role of antitrust counsel was more significant at Visa and MasterCard than at virtually any other large American corporation.

Many businesses can point to a period when antitrust concerns dominated their existence. The current AT&T is a smaller vestige of the old fully integrated Ma Bell. It was shaped and eventually split up in antitrust wars. Microsoft is still laboring under the influence of antitrust battles in the U.S., Europe and Asia. MCI, once the second largest telephone company in the U.S., would not have existed but for winning a huge antitrust case against AT&T in 1983. However, at Visa, the influence of antitrust has been constant. Heller Ehrman didn't get hired for each new matter, it was already there.

Such reflexive use of litigation counsel is foolish, regardless of how good the lawyers are. In addition to judging a firm's track record, a litigant should evaluate the plan for each specific case. Visa most likely neglected to do that. Heller Ehrman also brought additional baggage to this assignment. The law firm helped design the business and antitrust strategies under attack. They were not just defending Visa, they were defending themselves. As the old saying goes, "A lawyer who represents himself has a fool for a client."

The jubilation at Heller Ehrman, when C&P filed the merchants' complaint, was palpable. They would vindicate the legal and business strategy they had developed for Visa, and they would make a fortune doing it. Heller Ehrman immediately had celebratory hats made up that were inscribed, "HEWM Fit To Be Tied," a reference to the merchants' challenge of the Visa tying arrangement. John Wilke, a *Wall Street Journal* reporter who wrote numerous articles about the case throughout the seven years, heard about the hats and asked me to get one for him. When the case was over, I asked Brian Brosnahan, a brilliant HEWM litigator whom I had bonded with during the case, to get one of these hats for me. He perhaps misconstrued my request, although I doubt it, and sent a beautiful and expensive traditional hat. It was the type commonly worn by businessmen before the JFK inauguration relegated such hats to fashion antiquity. I sent him a beautiful shirt in return and asked again for the "Fit To Be Tied" baseball hat. He said that the hats had disappeared. I asked another Heller Ehrman lawyer for a hat and was told that those hats had never existed.

A&P, Visa's second law firm, technically played the role of "local counsel," because HEWM did not establish a New York office until 1999. A New York firm was a necessity for the Merchants' case, which was filed in federal court in Brooklyn. Such local counsel generally act as little more than a "mail drop" for the primary counsel. In this case, A&P wound up doing more depositions than lead counsel do in most big commercial cases. A&P did its job with the kind of professional dispassion that Visa needed and Heller Ehrman couldn't deliver because it was defending itself.

MasterCard retained Rogers & Wells to defend it. That firm was later acquired by, and became known as, Clifford Chance, the world's largest law firm. Clifford Chance adopted the same tactics as Heller Ehrman. They attempted to bury little C&P and succeeded in delaying the case. Clifford Chance, by and large, provided a generic representation for MasterCard. There were several exceptions. Briefly, and too late, Clifford Chance deployed Ken Gallo, who would have been the best trial lawyer on the defendants' side. They deployed Gallo so late, however, that the chances he would ever get to use his trial skills were slim, and eventually none.

From the outset, Clifford Chance assigned a special role to Kevin Arquit, or he may have assigned it to himself. Kevin, a handsome and charming guy from upstate New York, had been the General Counsel and Director of the Bureau of Competition of the FTC during parts of the Reagan and first Bush administrations. These were the years of the state/federal agency antitrust clash. I was the commander in chief for the states. Kevin was one of the opposing federal agency generals. We always respected each other and found time to step outside our roles, have a drink and laugh about the whole thing. He also danced with Jan at social occasions, as I suffer from a common male disease that allows me to play tournament-level tennis and squash, but prevents me from dancing. For more than six years, Kevin didn't take or defend a single deposition, or do much substantive work in the case, until January 10, 2003, the day we argued the enormous summary judgment motions. Until then, Kevin's job for MasterCard was to have lunch with me twice each year.

I told Kevin that I understood and appreciated why he regularly called to have a drink or a meal. Nobody expected this case to settle before trial. However, a settlement might occur after trial, if we were to win a monstrous monetary damage award. Against everyone's expectations, the case might even settle earlier. The day-to-day nastiness that quickly broke out between Clifford Chance and C&P, but which never occurred with Heller Ehrman or A&P, was not conducive to a settlement process. Kevin, whose greatest strength is his emotional intelligence, understood all this. He was out there implicitly saying, "If and when this case has to settle, you and I, who respect and like each other, will do it." And almost seven years later, that's the way it worked out.

Clifford Chance, Heller Ehrman, A&P and Simpson Thacher & Bartlett, who joined in MasterCard's defense toward the end, collectively had 5,839 lawyers. On top of that, the twenty-something banks that were on the Visa and MasterCard boards brought their own legions of lawyers. The banks were vitally concerned with the outcome of the Merchants' case, and both they and the networks asserted that the banks were legally entitled to come to the aid of Visa/MasterCard under a so-called "joint defense" privilege. If the court agreed that Visa, MasterCard and the banks could utilize this privilege, their communications in defense of the Merchants' case would remain secret, beyond the reach of our discovery demands. However, invoking this privilege on behalf of the two supposedly competing card networks and thousands of banks was another instance of Visa/MasterCard announcing to the world, "Hey, just in case you forgot, we are a fronting for a cartel, and this is a conspiracy."

Arrayed against these primary defense firms with their thousands of lawyers was my firm, Constantine & Partners. When the case was filed, C&P had eight lawyers, and when active hostilities ended seven years later we had grown to 17. Throughout these seven years of active litigation, 52 percent of C&P's resources were devoted to the case. But we had some very important help.

After C&P filed the Merchants' case as a class action, 29 other law firms representing 14 additional stores filed "copycat" lawsuits. We anticipated this and arranged for this to be done in an orderly and friendly way. Copycat lawsuits are filed by plaintiffs' firms in antitrust, securities and products liability cases after the government, or someone powerful like Wal-Mart, first files a case. The copycat complaints are usually identical to the first case except for the names of the new plaintiffs.

After the copycat lawsuits are filed, the court will usually "consolidate" the new complaints with the original lawsuit, creating a new "style" or name for the combined cases. After the copycat suits were filed and consolidated with the lawsuit we had filed for Wal-Mart and other giant merchants, the consolidated case was called "*In re VisaCheck/MasterMoney Antitrust Litigation.*" In most of these situations, the copycat lawsuits simply wait until the government or other lead plaintiff does all or most of the work, and if the lead plaintiff wins, the tag-along firms also collect damages for their clients and attorneys' fees for themselves. In the Merchants' case, I decided to enlist the assistance of the plaintiffs' firms who had filed the copycat cases. I reserved the vast majority of the complicated work for C&P, such as the court appearances, appeals, briefs, motions, expert reports and key depositions. C&P's big clients expected, and indeed demanded, that our firm do those tasks. They had hired us not those plaintiffs' firms who were constantly suing them in other class actions. But the firms who filed the copycat cases could assist with the many rudimentary but very time-consuming and important projects.

Before I "filed" the case (in important cases I personally do this chore), I knew that a class action complaint by Wal-Mart and The Limited would attract plaintiffs' class action firms to file virtually identical cases on behalf of clients whom they would come to represent, in a process that I neither understood nor particularly wanted to. The plaintiffs' class action bar, lead by firms such as Milberg Weiss and Hagens Berman, characteristically jump on a case filed by a government antitrust or securities agency. They quickly find a client with the same grievance as the plaintiffs in the first-filed case, and file nearly identical private lawsuits. They get organized and have lead counsel appointed through their own mechanisms or by court order. They then generally wait for the government case to develop facts and legal rulings, which they use to clean up in a process, which our judge, United States District Judge John Gleeson, later described as playing "jackals to the government's lion."

Knowing that the Wal-Mart/Limited complaint would attract these class action firms, just like a government lawsuit does, I brought one, Hagens Berman, into my confidence a month before our filing. I chose Hagens Berman, a firm based in Seattle, because one of its partners, George Sampson, was a person I could trust. George had been my deputy when I ran the New York Attorney General's Antitrust Bureau. Before that, George had worked with me in a Legal Services office in Brooklyn, where we represented poor people. My plan was for George's firm to file the first copycat case and then help us organize, control and utilize the resources of the other firms who would tag along.

Six days after we filed for Wal-Mart and The Limited, George's firm filed a copycat complaint on behalf of Bernie's Army Navy Store, located in Vineland, New Jersey. Eventually, three additional firms, none from New Jersey, joined in the representation of Bernie's, a sole proprietorship. Later, 25 additional firms joined in copycat filings on behalf of other stores. Most of these "law firms" were very small, and several had only one lawyer. Two of the copycat suits were filed for big retailers by larger plaintiffs' firms. Miller, Faucher filed for Burlington Coat Factory, and Milberg Weiss filed for Payless Shoe Source, the nation's largest shoe chain.

After the 14 copycat lawsuits were consolidated with C&P's lawsuit on behalf of Wal-Mart and the four other giant retailers, C&P was appointed lead counsel for the consolidated group of cases, which was a forgone conclusion. At my request, George's firm was appointed co-lead counsel to assist us. With George's help, we assigned very basic, but very important, work to the 29 other "firms" during the next seven years.

Constantine & Partners took care of the high-level work, a huge load for a small firm. We took or defended 80 percent of the roughly 400 depositions, where the litigants question likely trial witnesses and other people who have important evidence. This questioning is done under oath and stenographically recorded. With very important witnesses, the deposition is also videotaped. In many circumstances, these transcripts and videotapes are used at trial instead of live witness testimony. Six C&P partners—Gordon Schnell, Mitch Shapiro, Jeff Shinder, Matt Cantor, Stacey Mahoney and I—took or defended 270 of the 400 depositions. Other C&P partners and associates did many others. C&P wrote all the briefs in the district court, circuit court and United States Supreme Court. C&P argued all of the 350 motions. These motions involve pretrial disputes, such as whether a particular document can be withheld from the other side because it is asserted to be privileged. Some motions can completely end the case very early, such as a motion to dismiss the complaint. Other motions can end or reduce the size of the case before trial, such as a motion for "summary judgment."

C&P also prepared or responded to all 54 expert reports filed by the parties and deposed all 16 experts retained by Visa/MasterCard. As the Commander in Chief of our Army, I took or defended many of the crucial depositions, and did most of the major court arguments, including those resulting in our victories on the class action motion, the Second Circuit appeal of class certification; the summary judgment motions in the district court; and the defense of the settlement in the United States Court of Appeals for the Second Circuit.

On April 12, 1997, we filed the "operative" consolidated complaint in the Merchants' case. This document added C&P's new clients Sears, Safeway, Circuit City and the three large trade associations to the complaint we had previously filed on behalf of Wal-Mart and The Limited. It also consolidated the copycat plaintiffs and their law firms with our lead case and completed the team for a contest that would last six more years and beyond.

At that moment, I paused to assess what had taken ten years to coalesce from the epiphany about the Visa/MasterCard cartel on March 11, 1987, and six years to actively assemble from the time in 1991 when I had been retained by The Limited. This thing I had created scared me. That wasn't because I was afraid of losing, a result that viscerally never seemed likely to me. The fear came from investing so much time, past and future, in something I had planned.

At the age of 50, I had always taken pride in my ability to adapt to the unknown, and pleasure in not knowing what was just around the next curve. Confronting so much of my own, uncharacteristic, planning was unsettling to my self-image. For a moment, I thought of asking Jan and the kids to fulfill one of our frequently discussed fantasies of moving abroad for five years—maybe to London, Paris, Rome, or Sydney. The thought and the fear soon passed. I had built a law firm and a coalition of clients for this event, and I had promises to keep.

PART II

—

Six Battles

Among the thousands of skirmishes, six major battles, all won by the merchants, made the defendants' capitulation at the beginning of the trial a forgone conclusion. With each of these battles, a case that at the outset was widely viewed as impossible for the merchants to win, moved relentlessly toward a trial that virtually everybody thought Visa/MasterCard would not only lose, but might well result in their extinction. The defendants could never have paid the likely money verdict that would have been rendered by the jury after a trial that was shaped by these six defeats. The defeats left Visa/MasterCard virtually defenseless for the seventh battle, the trial itself.

In the first battle, a key argument and piece of evidence shifted the viewpoint of the magistrate judge from leaning to the defendants toward the arguments made by the merchants. That battle also resulted in Judge John Gleeson becoming active in the case, which, until then, had been primarily supervised by the assisting magistrate judge.

In the second battle, won by the merchants less than three weeks after the first, Judge Gleeson, now firmly in control of the case, granted the United States' motion to intervene in the Merchants' case so the government could get the benefit of the pretrial discovery and analyses that C&P had done. This created a legal and factual alliance between the merchants and the United States.

In the third battle, the five merchant-plaintiffs that had started the case became five million, as first Judge Gleeson, then the United States Court of Appeals for the Second Circuit, and finally the United States Supreme Court decided that the case should proceed as a class action on behalf of most of the country's merchants.

In the fourth battle, a key piece of evidence was made available to the merchants after a fight lasting 27 months. This single 50-page Visa document, whose cover was decorated with a shark, was almost as damaging to Visa/MasterCard as all the other documentary evidence culled from a record of some five million pages.

In the fifth battle, involving both sides' motions for summary judgment before trial, the merchants consolidated and capitalized on everything they had won in the first four battles. Judge Gleeson rejected all 14 motions made by Visa/MasterCard, granted most of the motions made by the merchants, and sent the plaintiffs into a trial in which most of the important disputes had already been decided in their favor.

The sixth battle, whose outcome was determined on the day a jury was picked and trial was about to begin, involved a series of "Hail Mary" passes hurled by Visa/MasterCard on the eve of trial. These desperate efforts were made in an attempt to claw back most of what they had lost in the first five key battles. These frantic attempts were defeated.

Certainly, there were other important battles, some involving the defendants' consistent success at getting the district court, circuit court and Supreme Court to delay the case to the point where it went to trial three-and-a-half years after it should have. Another major contest resulted in the district court's rejection of the defendants' attempt to sanction Wal-Mart and dismiss it from the case for what the defendants alleged was Wal-Mart's destruction of relevant evidence during the discovery process. Nevertheless, these six battles were the most crucial.

The Tide Turns

IN DECEMBER 1999, the parties were ordered to attend a so-called "settlement conference" supervised by Magistrate Judge Roanne Mann, who was Judge Gleeson's helper for this case. John Gleeson, our judge, was a tough, handsome (I am told by my wife) former chief of the U.S. Attorney's Criminal Division in the Eastern District of New York, whose main courthouse is located in downtown Brooklyn. John Gleeson is the man who put mafia boss John Gotti behind bars after a relentless, but previously futile, pursuit by federal prosecutors. The failed prosecutions before the successful one led by Gleeson had earned Gotti the nickname "the Teflon Don." Gleeson, like many federal judges, relies heavily on magistrate judges to assist him and handle the many pretrial disputes that arise in big commercial cases.

Magistrate Judge Roanne ("Ronnie") Mann, is a very smart, but humorless jurist whom I never caught smiling (at least at me) in the seven active years of the Merchants' case. She was assigned the task of managing the pretrial discovery process in which each party can obtain documents and other evidence from the opposing party and from non-parties who have relevant information. Magistrate Judge Mann also handled the mundane disputes that arose frequently during that tedious process. The parties briefed and argued an astounding

350 motions during the course of the litigation. Most of these motions involved discovery disputes. Mediating and, when necessary, ruling on these disputes was an important task that Mann did well.

In early 1997, Magistrate Judge Mann established a schedule for discovery, involving the exchange of documents, the taking of depositions and the asking and answering of written questions called "interrogatories" and "requests for admission." She also scheduled a settlement conference for December 15, 1998. She picked this date to coincide with the expected final days of discovery. Mann did this so the parties would come to the settlement conference with a serious and sober understanding of how much evidence each side had to support its case.

The settlement conference was delayed one full year until December 1999, because Mann extended the fact discovery deadline from December 1998 until March 2000. Despite the obvious fact that the defendants had enough lawyers to fill an arena, the magistrate judge consistently granted their requests for more time to take discovery and perform other pretrial tasks. Her accommodation of the defendants' requests for delay made the case years longer and much more expensive and raised the question of whether we could ever prevail. "Justice delayed is justice denied."

Even more troubling than these delays was the Magistrate Judge's ruling on the parties' competing motions about the scope of discovery. The guidelines for discovery in federal civil cases set the presumptive limit on depositions at *ten* for each side. The guidelines for complex litigation—and our case was nothing if not complex—suggests the number can be doubled to *20* depositions for each side. We knew that Heller Ehrman, A&P and Clifford Chance were trying to bury us and would try to get the court's approval for many more than the presumptive 40 depositions. We also realized that some expansion beyond 20 per side was not only likely but reasonable, given the virtually unprecedented size of the case. So, to preempt the defendants, we proposed a shocking number of depositions, 300, almost eight times the presumptive limit, to be divided equally. We also proposed that most depositions be limited to one day. To give the reader some frame of reference on our proposal, consider that in the massive *Microsoft* antitrust case being litigated in the same timeframe, and sharing some of the same experts and theories as our earlier-filed case, the judge limited the number of depositions to 93.

The defendants opposed our proposal, saying 300 depositions were not enough. Frankly, I thought that Magistrate Judge Mann would chastise all the parties—us for proposing an excessive number, and the defendants for rejecting it. To our amazement, Mann agreed with the defendants and refused to put any limit on the number of depositions. She also rejected our proposed one-day limitation on the duration of most depositions. The result was 400 depositions, a number astounding to any lawyer who has heard it. Many of these depositions lasted two or three days, and one went on for almost six.

"Double-tracking" depositions means holding two depositions on the same day. Many courts require permission for double-tracking because, among other things, a big firm can overwhelm a small firm by double- or triple-tracking depositions. Because of the magistrate judge's refusal to meaningfully control the discovery process, we had many days with four, five and six depositions, several days with seven and one day with nine depositions, occurring simultaneously all over the U.S.

Rather than appeal Magistrate Judge Mann's ruling to Judge Gleeson, we decided to turn it to our advantage. Our little firm wound up taking considerably more depositions than the defendants did with their massive law firms. More importantly, the depositions we took were incredibly effective. Most of these were videotaped and revealed not just everything we had alleged, but much more.

In one deposition, MasterCard executive Ed Hogan, a former FBI official, blurted out that Visa and MasterCard had agreed to remove "MasterCard II" and "Electron," the names of their debit card programs, from the face of their debit cards. Without these markings, merchants and consumers could not readily distinguish debit cards from credit cards. Startling admissions, like the one made by Mr. Hogan, are supposed to occur as the result of long and skillful questioning by the lawyer. You take the witness through a series of questions designed to corner him or her. You then ask a question that can only be answered truthfully with the information you want, or with a lie. The lie, if detected, would damage the credibility of the witness and could be used at trial to hurt the opposing party. I wish I could claim that my skillful questioning elicited this admission from former Special Agent Hogan, but in fact he just blurted it out. There is a deep-seated human need to confess.

As the discovery process reached its final months, and we prepared for the settlement conference, we were confident that we had uncovered a treasure trove of information that was damning to the defendants. However, we still continued to be wary of Magistrate Judge Mann, who had authorized the excessive "all you can eat" approach to discovery and had granted the defendants' requests to seriously delay the case.

To prepare for the settlement conference, we held a meeting of our direct clients—the five big stores and the three trade associations. We flew into O'Hare and met at the Airport Hilton, where I showed the plaintiffs' in-house counsel the best of the best evidence against the defendants. We then established settlement demands that we would make at the conference. Given the strength of the evidence, neither we nor our clients were inclined to compromise very much. The magistrate judge later told us that our demands were ludicrous. A comparison of the demands we made in December 1999 with what we ultimately settled for, reveals that the actual settlement provided for significantly more relief.

The settlement conference began on December 14, 1999, three months before the then scheduled end of discovery. The conference was held in the old United States Courthouse in downtown Brooklyn, in a cramped auxiliary courtroom of the kind assigned to magistrate judges. Twenty-nine lawyers from both sides shoehorned our way into the little courtroom, making the ballpark estimate of billable time for each and every hour of the two-day conference $15,000. All the heavy hitters from both sides were there, except one notable and anticipated (by me) exception, that of Bob Norton, MasterCard's General Counsel. He continued his practice of absenting himself from places where I would be.

I was nervous but confident, having prepared for my presentation of the merchants' compelling evidence by making a similar six-hour presentation to our clients at the O'Hare Airport Hilton meeting a few weeks before. The mountain of evidence supporting our case was summarized for the magistrate judge in a 720-page binder that C&P had compiled. The defendants made a similar, submission, showing what they considered their most compelling evidence.

I believed that the magistrate judge had a slightly negative view of our case going into the conference. This impression was primarily based upon her rulings during the previous three years. She had accommodated the defendants' dilatory tactics, and most of her rulings had gone against us. However, given the fact that the majority of these rulings were procedural, such as those dealing with the number and length of depositions, this in and of itself did not say much. In fact, judges tend to make procedural rulings against the side that is winning. They do this to eliminate certain bases for appeal and for subtle, but understandable, psychological reasons. Parents often give the larger allowance to the less-favored child. The skepticism

I perceived emanating from Magistrate Judge Mann was about the substance of our case and involved Visa/MasterCard's main steering defense. I sensed that she found persuasive Visa/MasterCard's argument that virtually all of the damage we complained of could easily be eliminated by a store steering the shopper to use another form of payment. "Miss Jones, I'd rather you pay some other way."

At the outset of the conference, the Magistrate invited the parties to present some of their strongest evidence and best arguments. I seized the podium and, in a virtual soliloquy that would have impressed Fidel Castro, I spoke for almost four hours without stopping. In truth, there were some questions from the bench, but not very many. Those few were not challenging but merely asked for some clarification of a point or piece of evidence I had just presented.

I talked about some of the most probative documentary and deposition evidence. This was the evidence that would prove our case and rebut Visa/MasterCard's defenses. My presentation that day was organized in the same way that I made every such presentation during the course of this case. It followed the elements of the two main claims in the Merchants' case, that Visa/MasterCard were illegally tying debit to credit and attempting to monopolize the debit card market. Each of these two claims had four parts or "elements" that we had to prove. The evidence I showed tended to prove each element in their order, such as that credit cards and debit cards were different products and that Visa and MasterCard each and collectively had "market power" in the credit card market. All of this was being disputed by the defendants. My style of "building block" presentation may seem obvious and common. It's not. Lawyers like to show juries and judges "hot documents," which cast the opposing party in a very bad light. I think it's a waste of time to prove that Visa executives are cheating on their spouses unless that is an element of a practice violating the antitrust laws. On December 14, 1999, I went into court with an abundance of riches. The evidence I wielded was not only highly probative of each element of our claims but also very hot. The defendants were not cheating on their spouses, but they were beating up my clients in a manner that violated the antitrust laws. In addition to presenting this evidence, which "proved" our case, I tried to anticipate the arguments the defendants would make, that is, if I ever actually would sit down. I also tried to preempt what I knew would be Visa and MasterCard's presentation about steering, but left a few juicy items in reserve.

The defendants spoke for less than two hours and used the bulk of this time to talk about their steering defense. They ignored the evidence I had just presented, showing that merchants couldn't steer for two reasons: first, because the defendants had disguised the identity of their debit cards, and second, because the defendants' rules prohibited it. In the face of all this, they argued about the ease and ubiquity of steering customers away from using debit cards, but with virtually no documentary support. This seemed to jar the magistrate, whose facial expression and body language subtly changed right in front of us. The fact that this change was subtle was less significant than that her demeanor changed at all. Ronnie Mann's job was to get the parties to settle, and any hint from her that gave either party confidence would run counter to her objective.

Then, in rebuttal, I got up and showed a video clip from the deposition of Pete Hart, the former CEO of MasterCard, who had left that position in March 1994. Hart had been the MasterCard CEO during the aftermath of the states' lawsuit terminating the Entrée debit card network. At the time, Hart as much as said that the death of Entrée would stimulate the growth of the debit card market. Soon after, Hart tried to get MasterCard to adopt a debit card strategy different from Visa's. Visa called on the banks that owned both MasterCard and Visa to force MasterCard to reverse course. Soon after this episode Hart left MasterCard, and MasterCard did change direction, joining with Visa in the anticompetitive practices that formed the core of our case.

Pete Hart was a very likeable man. He was handsome and courtly, had captained the football team at Harvard, and also had a brief stint as an end with the Boston Patriots in the old American Football League. After we filed the case, a mutual acquaintance in the industry suggested that I meet with Hart. This friend thought that Hart might agree to testify for the merchants, given the fact that Hart's position on debit while at MasterCard was similar to the one we were asserting in the Merchants' case. Considering Hart's stature and previous position with MasterCard, such testimony would likely have been very damaging to the defendants' case. Although we had never met personally, Hart took my call, knowing exactly who I was, and quickly agreed to meet with me a few weeks later. I traveled to Philadelphia, where Hart lived. We spent a day discussing the Merchants' case, and I asked him to testify about his knowledge of whether Visa had forced MasterCard to reverse its debit strategy and whether he had been forced out of MasterCard because of this episode. He said he would think about it, but his closing comment suggested that his ultimate answer would be no. He said he was well off and didn't need work in the industry, but that one of his children might want a job. He said that his testimony could be a problem for her. He never got back to me and arrived at his deposition several months later with five lawyers, all paid for by MasterCard, representing him. Three of these lawyers were in-house counsel for MasterCard and he also had two outside lawyers he had retained from Steptoe & Johnson.

During the two days that I deposed him, Hart, surrounded by his legal battalion, surrendered so much testimony damaging to the defendants' case that showing the jury the video of this testimony would have proven more damaging for defendants than the friendly testimony I had attempted to obtain from him. Some of this damning testimony was predictable, as it was well known that Hart had been a champion of the superior PIN debit product and had criticized the security, functionality and pricing of signature debit cards. There was little doubt in my mind that Pete Hart had been forced out of MasterCard in 1994 because of these heresies. However, the most devastating testimony in Hart's deposition concerned the Visa/MasterCard steering defense. I only showed the magistrate judge a small portion of this on December 14, 1999, and later showed the same clip in open court for the summary judgment argument on January 10, 2003.

In the video clip, Hart testified that MasterCard's rules prohibited the steering that the defendants were relying upon as their magic bullet. If steering customers toward using another form of payment was prohibited by MasterCard's own rules, then this main line of defense in the case would fall apart. The video showed the defendants asking for a break after Hart made this damning admission.

When the deposition resumed, Hart said he wanted to correct his previous testimony and stated that the steering, which he had said was prohibited by MasterCard's rule, had, in fact, been allowed when he was CEO. Pete Hart, the epitome of Ivy League cool, looked uncomfortable and bewildered. I asked him what had caused him to change his testimony, and he said that he had a conversation during the break with Noah Hanft, MasterCard's "U.S. Counsel" and now its General Counsel. Hart testified that Hanft had told him, "Pete, you're confused a little around then." I quickly took Hart through a series of questions about his changed testimony. He got more and more flustered and confused and repeatedly said that his revised testimony was due to his conversation with Noah Hanft. He said this nine times.

When I showed this clip to the magistrate judge in front of the defendants, she became visibly angry but said nothing. The subtlety in her change in demeanor was gone. She asked me why a merchant couldn't distinguish a Visa or MasterCard debit card from a credit card. Reaching into my back pocket for my wallet, I pulled my ATM card out and handed it to her. I had a Chase ATM/debit card with a MasterCard logo on the front. It had a peel-off sticker that read: "IMPORTANT—THIS CARD IS NOT A CREDIT CARD. IT IS YOUR NEW CHASE BANKING CARD…." I explained that the sticker was there to warn the cardholder that what appeared to be a MasterCard credit card was, in fact, a debit card. I pointed out that when the cardholder removed the sticker, as Chase instructed, the actual nature of the card would remain unknown to the merchant. It seemed that a light went on in the magistrate judge's head. After watching the Hart video and the card demonstration, Magistrate Mann clearly tilted toward us. I can't prove it, but I strongly believe that she communicated her impressions to Judge Gleeson. The balance of the two-day conference was spent with the magistrate judge attempting shuttle diplomacy and hearing the oral argument of five motions that had been briefed by the parties but hadn't been decided. Most of these motions were procedural in nature, involving the flow of information between the Merchants' case and the U.S. case against Visa/MasterCard, pending in the Southern District courthouse two miles away. One motion involved a request by the defendants for yet another delay, and there also was one important motion concerning the legal status of communications between Visa/MasterCard and their banks.

The clearest signal of Magistrate Judge Mann's tilt toward our position came during the argument of that last motion. The motion concerned the so-called joint defense privilege that Visa/MasterCard and their banks were asserting. Under a joint defense privilege, the conversations of two separate parties about defending a case are privileged in the same way that the conversations between a lawyer and client are. Visa/MasterCard's argument was that we should not be able to ask bank executives about their conversations with Visa or MasterCard concerning the case. When lawyers for the defendants made this argument, Magistrate Judge Mann angrily asked them questions that referred to what she had seen in the video clip from Pete Hart's deposition. She adverted to what she sarcastically called "more subtle prompting" in response to an argument made by Visa's lawyer about communications between banks and Visa. Understanding that this sarcastic comment was directed at MasterCard and the Hart deposition clip, two MasterCard lawyers jumped up and tried to put their best spin on what Mann had seen and obviously been angered by. They also explained that Noah Hanft wasn't MasterCard's General Counsel, he was their "U.S. Counsel." As if that mattered.

Finally, the defendants asked for another delay on top of the 15 months that the magistrate judge had already granted. Jim Benedict, MasterCard's lead lawyer, rationalized the request with a reverse David and Goliath—inaccurately stating that the defendants had only two firms against our "20, 30." He was referring to C&P's 29 helper firms, several of which were one-lawyer firms.

Things were never quite the same after that day. Every major battle after that was resolved resoundingly in our favor. Immediately after the settlement conference, the motions argued the second day were decided in our favor. The magistrate judge consulted with Judge Gleeson, who denied the defendants' request for a further delay. In the two months after the conference, Judge Gleeson took hold of a case that, up to that point, he had primarily delegated to the magistrate judge's care. In that two-month period, the merchants won two more of the six key battles. Next up was the United States' motion to intervene in the Merchants' case, so the U.S. could have all the evidence revealed in the discovery phase of our case and, more importantly, get all the analyses of evidence that C&P had done in the previous three years.

The U.S. Hitches a Ride

IN THE YEAR prior to C&P filing the complaint, and during the two years after, I had a series of meetings with the FTC, numerous state attorneys general and the federal Antitrust Division. Among the many government officials I met with were FTC Chairman Bob Pitofsky and Joel Klein, who soon would become the head of the federal Antitrust Division. As described earlier, these meetings concerned the merchants' complaints about the tying arrangements and other alleged Visa/MasterCard antitrust violations. We urged the government agencies to pursue some of these claims in cases of their own.

In October 1998, two years after we filed the Merchants' case, the Antitrust Division filed its own case in the Manhattan-based United States District Court for the Southern District of New York. The Southern District courthouse is within moderate walking distance of the Eastern District in Brooklyn, where our case was proceeding.

The primary focus of the United States' case was different than ours, but much of the proof and economic theory necessary for the U.S. to win its case was similar to that necessary for us to win ours. The United States claimed, as we had previously, that Visa and MasterCard's exclusionary rules suppressed competition from

American Express, Discover and others by barring their banks from issuing American Express or Discover brand credit or debit cards or the cards of any other network that Visa/MasterCard considered to be a competitor. The United States' case focused on how these rules, Visa By-law 2.10(e) and MasterCard's "Competitive Programs Policy," injured competition in the credit card market. Our focus had been on how these rules injured competition in the debit card market. Because Visa's rule exempted MasterCard, and MasterCard's rule exempted Visa, both rules screamed, "Hey, Visa and MasterCard are not really competitors."

The U.S. also attacked Visa/MasterCard duality, but only in a limited and trivial way. The Antitrust Division didn't attack the dual ownership of Visa and MasterCard by the same banks, nor the practice of most major banks that issued both Visa and MasterCard credit cards. The U.S. only attacked what they called "governance duality," where a bank like Citibank sat on the board of Visa while serving on a governing body at MasterCard, such as its so-called "Business Committee," and thereby exercised a significant role in running both companies simultaneously. The Merchants' case also claimed that governance duality was anticompetitive, but only in conjunction with dual ownership and card-issuing duality.

The government limited, hampered and eventually lost this claim for two reasons. First, the Antitrust Division was still trying to rationalize its 1975 error of encouraging duality in the first place. Second, the division harbored an honest, but misguided, fear that if banks were forced to choose affiliation with only one association, virtually all would abandon MasterCard and flock to Visa. The division feared a result in which the tightly coordinated Visa/MasterCard "duopoly" would be replaced by a Visa monopoly. The fear was misguided because it essentially reflected a lack of trust in competition. In the ensuing years, when banks made choices to do business primarily with either MasterCard or Visa, under so-called "dedication agreements," MasterCard did very well.

Soon after the U.S. filed its case in October 1998, it moved to intervene in the Merchants' case, in order to get access to the evidence we had obtained in the discovery process and the thousands of hours of analysis C&P had done concerning the legal and factual issues common to both cases. We also wanted the U.S. to have our analyses, which were protected by the so-called "attorney work product" privilege. Visa and MasterCard didn't want the Antitrust Division to have the benefit of our work product and opposed their getting it unless they also got it. We couldn't allow the defendants to get access to these analyses because they were a detailed blueprint of our case and trial strategy.

The parties submitted legal briefs to Judge Gleeson on these issues in March 1999. On January 3, 2000, Judge Gleeson ruled for the government and the merchants in a decision of first impression, meaning on a point of law that had not previously been ruled on by any court. He ruled that we could give our analyses to the Antitrust Division without waiving their privileged status. We turned over to the Antitrust Division virtually everything we had done, and later on, everything we did. We assigned several lawyers to cull the entire file to find documents, deposition extracts, facts and analyses that could assist the U.S. One C&P lawyer, Mike Spyropolous, was assigned to do this, and virtually nothing else, for more than a year. He began the process of accumulating information helpful to the U.S. even before Judge Gleeson issued his ruling. We wanted to hit the ground running when, and if, Judge Gleeson made a favorable ruling. We wanted to help the U.S. get to trial as fast as possible and win its case.

Our motives were both public-spirited and selfish. We wanted the U.S. to win and win fast. Many of the issues that the U.S. had to establish were similar or identical to issues we had to establish in order to win our case. For example, for the U.S. to win its exclusionary rules claim, it had to prove that there was a credit card market and rebut the defendants' claim that credit cards were just a small part of the much bigger payment market that included cash, checks, debit cards and wampum. We also had to prove that there was a separate credit card market in order to establish a tying arrangement between two distinct products—credit cards and debit cards. There were many other issues, facts, points of law, witnesses and themes common to the two cases.

Despite its start two years after us, the U.S. was very likely to get to trial first. The government's case was much smaller. The judge and magistrate judge in that case were less willing to grant Visa and MasterCard time extensions, and federal courts also generally expedite proceedings in which the U.S. is the plaintiff. If, as expected, the U.S. were to get to trial first, and win on some of the legal issues common to both cases, we could get the benefit of such rulings under a doctrine called "collateral estoppel." The collateral estoppel rule does not work in the opposite direction, meaning that if the U.S. were to lose on these common issues, we would not be bound by those negative rulings.

I thought it very likely that the judges in the two cases would find each other's rulings persuasive. Judge Gleeson headed the Criminal Division of the U.S. Attorneys Office in the Eastern District during the same time period that Judge Barbara Jones, the judge in the U.S. case, had run the Criminal Division in the Southern District, only two miles away. They both had gained recognition as organized crime prosecutors. Gleeson had successfully prosecuted John Gotti. Jones had been part of a multi-agency task force that had prosecuted the Mafia "Commission" cases that, parenthetically, had utilized the "Sal Avellino Black Jaguar" bugs, which are famous in law enforcement circles. These recordings of Luchese crime family

Five Merchants
Become Five Million

A CRUCIAL THIRD HURDLE was to have Judge Gleeson grant our motion to certify a class of five million U.S. merchants, and then successfully defend that decision in the Court of Appeals and the United States Supreme Court. The certification of the class would raise the monetary stakes in the case from hundreds of millions of dollars to billions and potentially tens of billions. Both sides knew that the outcome of the class motion would not only change the defendants' damage exposure by a factor of more than ten, but psychologically buoy the winners and crush the losers. More work was devoted to this single motion than is done in the entirety of most large and complex commercial cases.

We petitioned for class certification in April 1999 and were disappointed that Judge Gleeson assigned this crucial motion to Magistrate Judge Mann for initial determination. At the time, we were very unhappy with the magistrate judge. She had delayed the case by more than a year, extending the fact discovery deadline from December 1998 to March 2000. She had rejected what we thought was our absurdly preemptive proposal of limiting discovery to 300 depositions, allowing the parties instead to engage in an "all you can eat" discovery orgy. Most of her rulings, primarily procedural, were going against us, and she was making them impatiently and slowly—an annoying combination. We really couldn't do anything about Judge Gleeson handing off the class action motion to Magistrate Judge Mann, but vainly protest and alienate her. So we didn't.

Our concerns about the Magistrate Judge deciding the crucial class motion had already been partially validated as we went before her for the December 14–15, 1999, settlement conference. This date was eight full months after the motion was filed, and five months after it had been fully briefed by the parties. Nevertheless, Magistrate Judge Mann hadn't even scheduled oral argument of the motion, let alone decided it. After the settlement conference and the attitude shift that we witnessed from her, the class motion was immediately returned to Judge Gleeson. Although this was done without explanation, we were sure that we understood the significance of this act. After the parties convinced the magistrate judge that settlement discussions were pointless, she told both sides that the respective settlement demands were ludicrous. At a separate meeting with us, she asked (and therefore probably asked Visa/MasterCard at their separate meeting) what we believed would get the other side to bargain in good faith. I responded that speedy argument and determination of the class motion would probably do that. I believe that the magistrate judge conveyed this message to Judge Gleeson. Right after that conference, Judge Gleeson took the motion back from the magistrate judge and scheduled oral argument.

The case within the case that this class motion proved to be produced several incidents that showed me how defense counsel, if not the defendants, were beginning to panic and crumble. The first incident involved the defendants' selection and use of an economist in their efforts to defeat the class motion. The defendants' counsel, and principally Heller Ehrman, attempted to defeat the class motion by staging a premature duel of expert economists. Battles between expert witnesses, such as economists, usually occur during the trial or just before the trial during a motion process called "summary judgment." In the Merchants' case the defendants chose to stage this fight during the class motion, years before trial.

Law has its fashions, like cuisine and fashion itself. Just as "handcrafted" and "artisanal" foods and long, severely pointed women's shoes are currently in fashion, "*Daubert* motions" are the defense tactic of the moment in complex litigation, especially in antitrust cases. In a *Daubert* motion, named after a 1993 Supreme Court decision, a party attacks the opposing expert witness on the ground that the expert's report or testimony amounts to "junk science." The doctrine applies when a false science such as, say, phrenology (the interpretation of human head contours) or alchemy is offered to support the party's case. The *Daubert* doctrine also applies when a "science" like physics or economics is offered in a bogus manner, or using flawed methodology.

Instead of using the *Daubert* doctrine as the Supreme Court intended, to prevent an impressionable jury from being swayed by phony science or flawed methodology, defense counsel now routinely make a *Daubert* motion against most opposing experts, even those highly credentialed. The doctrine is now flagrantly overused and abused, especially in attacks on economists. In fairness, it should be said that the squishiness of economic science and the ease with which a well-healed company can find an economist to support virtually any business practice, no matter how venal, has invited such frequent "junk science" attacks. Truly talented economists with great integrity have suffered in this process.

Heller Ehrman was in the vanguard of this fashionable defense tactic. They were to *Daubert* motions what Dolce and Gabbana are to pointy women's shoes. Heller Ehrman had packaged a *Daubert* motion program and actively marketed, to corporate counsel, its ability to knock out plaintiffs' experts at legal and economic conferences. One of these conferences is held annually at the fancy Bishop's Lodge dude ranch in Santa Fe, New Mexico, by the National Economic Research Associates, or "NERA," a subsidiary of Marsh & McLennan. At this conference, held each year in early July, antitrust lawyers and their significant others are NERA's all-expenses-paid guests for ridin', ropin', square dancin', the Santa Fe Opry and drinkin' with NERA economists, who typically charge 1,000 buckaroos per hour to act as experts in antitrust cases. I was the lead speaker at this conference in 1989, three weeks before filing the *Entrée* case. The antitrust cases I was pursuing, and the business practices NERA's economists were justifying with expert testimony, began to collide. As will be seen, the biggest collision occurred in the Merchants' case.

In April 1999, we filed our motion for class certification, asserting that the same Visa/MasterCard rules and contracts that coerced Wal-Mart, Sears, Circuit City, Safeway and The Limited to accept Visa/MasterCard debit card transactions similarly coerced the millions of other U.S. merchants in the proposed class. We alleged that class members had all been injured by paying more for Visa/MasterCard debit transactions than if they had been able to negotiate a price for debit card acceptance untied from Visa/MasterCard credit card acceptance. We submitted proof that every one of the millions of stores in the class had purchased credit and debit card services from Visa/MasterCard under identical contractual provisions.

We also supported our motion with an expert report from Professor Dennis Carlton. Carlton is a famous economist from the University of Chicago whose values and integrity are such that when his consulting firm won a defamation action against a plaintiffs' antitrust firm, Dennis donated his entire million-dollar share to charity. The purpose of Professor Carlton's report was to show how the millions of stores in the class all suffered similar monetary injury, which could be calculated for each store using the same simple formula. Professor Carlton didn't say that the amount of damage suffered by all stores was the same, only that all stores' damages were of a similar nature and could be calculated using the same formula.

Professor Carlton's expert report also said that the tying arrangements and other anticompetitive conduct had raised the price of signature debit transactions. He reasoned that without the defendants' conduct, the price of signature debit would have been lower, as it has been since the Merchants' case was settled, ending the tie between debit and credit. Carlton demonstrated that if the tying arrangements raised prices by, say, $1.00 for each $100.00 in debit transaction dollar volume, then it would be simple to calculate each class member's monetary damage. If a merchant had been forced to accept only $100 in debit transactions, its damage would be $1.00. If a merchant had been forced to accept $100,000.00 in debit transactions, its damage would be $1,000.00. I am simplifying Carlton's report and formula, but not by much. The theory was simple, logical and, most importantly, based on facts.

Heller Ehrman decided to attack Professor Carlton, utilizing their prefabricated *Daubert* motion tactic and employing one of NERA's most renowned economists, Dr. Richard Schmalensee, the Dean of the Sloan School of Management at MIT. In 1999, the case was years away from having a jury who needed protection from what the defendants claimed was Professor Carlton's junk science. Nevertheless, Visa and MasterCard filed a *Daubert* motion, telling Judge Gleeson that he (not a jury) must be protected from naively relying upon Carlton's report. Carlton, the author of many scholarly books and articles, is so well regarded in the antitrust field that he was one of only two outside economists consulted by the Antitrust Division and the FTC in the formulation of their merger enforcement guidelines. Later, in 2006, he became the Antitrust Division's chief economist.

The other outside economist who consulted on the federal agencies' merger guidelines was Dean Schmalensee, a plain-spoken, but intensely intellectual, teacher and eminent industrial organization economist. Heller Ehrman "retained" NERA and Dean Schmalensee to be their economic consultants on the class motion and to attack Carlton. In truth, just as Heller Ehrman is not really retained by Visa for each antitrust case, neither was Schmalensee really retained by Heller Ehrman. He was already there. Visa and Heller Ehrman had previously used Schmalensee in the 1991 *Mountainwest* case, where Discover sued Visa, in the United States' 1998 case against Visa, and another antitrust case called *Valley Bank v. Visa.*

After we filed the Merchants' case in 1996, Visa commissioned Schmalensee and Dr. David Evans, his NERA colleague, to write a book called *Paying with Plastic,* which attempted to justify the practices that were the subjects of the Merchants' case and the case against Visa/MasterCard, which the U.S. government was likely to file, and later did. I looked forward to cross-examining Schmalensee about his book at trial. It was published replete with the Dean's thanks and acknowledgments to Visa's General Counsel and the lawyers at Heller Ehrman. It seemed that Visa and Heller Ehrman had the same idea as we had at C&P, meaning: "If you do everything, you will win." But in my mind, paying for a book to be written by an economist who will be your expert fell into the category of doing everything to make sure you will lose. Experts are supposed to approach their assignments without preconceived conclusions and with the ability to maintain scientific objectivity.

Dean Schmalensee arrived in Boston during the spring of 1999 for his task of discrediting Professor Carlton, with a major handicap. It wasn't fatigue from the trip across the Charles River in Cambridge, where MIT is located. At that moment, Schmalensee was over-whelmed by his obligations as Microsoft's economist in the antitrust case that the U.S. and 21 state attorneys general were pressing against the computer software monopolist. In that case, the lead economist for the United States was Dr. Franklin Fisher, also an economics pro-fessor at MIT.

Professor Fisher was also our lead economist in the Merchants' case, having been retained for our assignment a year before beginning his work on the *Microsoft* case. Frank Fisher is a handsome septua-genarian with a full crown of brilliant white hair. He has served as the lead economist in many of the most important antitrust cases of the last half century, including the *IBM* case, which the Reagan Antitrust Division abandoned after a dozen years of hard work by previous administrations. After we hired Frank, he began his work as chief economist in *Microsoft*. Fisher had been retained by the U.S. to oppose his MIT protégé, Dick Schmalensee. Schmalensee had been "retained" by Heller Ehrman to oppose his mentor, Professor Fisher, in our case. This double *mano a mano* was not coincidental.

Fisher and Schmalensee are two of a small number of the elite industrial organization economists likely to testify in antitrust cases of the magnitude of the Merchants' case and *Microsoft*. These two cases shared many similarities. The Merchants' case was premised on the assertion that Visa/MasterCard, which were already domi-nant in credit cards, were leveraging their monopoly power into the newer debit card market through tying arrangements and other predatory conduct. Nineteen months later, the *Microsoft* suit alleged that Microsoft was leveraging its operating system monopoly power into the market for Internet browsers, where its Internet Explorer browser had been a distant second to Netscape's Navigator browser. After tying the Internet Explorer browser to Windows, Microsoft's browser quickly became dominant. Microsoft achieved this dominance because of the tying arrangement and other anticompetitive conduct. It was nice, or as economists say, it was "efficient" for the U.S. to have Professor Fisher develop his theory of tying predation on somebody else's dime. For us, that "dime" eventually amounted to $7,355,071.33, which was the fee we paid to Charles River Associates, Professor Fisher's economic consulting firm.

C&P, unlike Heller Ehrman, decided not to expose its chief economist at the class motion stage of the Merchants' case. We wanted to see how the Fisher versus Schmalensee duel played out in the *Microsoft* case first. Despite being filed after the Merchant case, the *Microsoft* case would get to trial much faster. It was a government case, there was no jury, and all affirmative testimony was done in writing with live and videotaped cross-examination. Moreover, despite the media circus, the *Microsoft* case was a smaller case than ours. In terms of the logistics alone, the Microsoft judge had wisely limited the number of depositions to 93 and the number of trial witnesses to 24, compared to the nearly 400 depositions and the 730 potential trial witnesses listed in our pretrial order.

Not only was Heller Ehrman exposing Schmalensee before his performance in the *Microsoft* case could be fully assessed, I already had most of his *Microsoft* testimony in written form and could explore and exploit any inconsistencies between what he said about tying arrangements in that case and what he said about the same subject in our case. I was going to get two shots at deposing and discrediting Schmalensee, once at the class motion stage and again after his final liability and damage reports were filed in our case and after the *Microsoft* outcome was known. I wasn't going to give Visa/ MasterCard the same chance against Professor Fisher. So, we used Professor Carlton at the class motion stage, reserving Fisher for the actual trial.

After we filed our class motion supported by Professor Carlton's short expert report, the defendants opposed the motion and also moved to disqualify Carlton under the *Daubert* junk science doctrine. Visa and MasterCard jointly filed a 91-page report, allegedly authored by Dean Schmalensee, to support their position. We had charged that Visa and MasterCard didn't really compete and should be viewed as a two-headed monopolist. However, they claimed to be fierce competitors. What did they do to demonstrate this fierce rivalry? They jointly filed Schmalensee's expert report, replete with statements like "virtually all of the statements I make for Visa are true for MasterCard as well."

From the earliest moments of his deposition, Dick Schmalensee, in the manner of that other Dick, made certain things perfectly clear. He was very tired, busy and preoccupied with the *Microsoft* case, which would resume trial in only a few weeks. He testified that he had spent no more than 30 hours working on the Merchants' case, including work on the liability part of the case prior to our filing the class motion. This meant he had spent considerably less than 30 hours on "his" 91-page expert report with 189 footnotes.

It is hard for me to conceive of an economist writing a scholarly report of this length and density in 30 hours let alone less than that, and Schmalensee, to his credit, quickly admitted that he hadn't written it. Colleagues at NERA had written the report, and he had signed it. He also admitted that he hadn't interviewed a single Visa or MasterCard executive.

I asked him to explain what was meant when his report said that *"virtually all of the statements I make for Visa, are true for MasterCard as well."* Schmalensee was surprised that the report covered Master-Card as well as Visa and admitted that "I worked on it without any notion of what MasterCard might or might not do." Dean Schmalensee even admitted that he didn't know that he was acting as MasterCard's expert until I pointed this out to him during the deposition.

This was just preliminary fun. The admissions that Schmalensee made about the substance of the report were even more injurious to the defendants' position. I asked Schmalensee about his report's attack on the economic model used by our economist, Dennis Carlton, who was the Dean's coconsultant on the federal merger guidelines. He answered that "I simply haven't done enough study to have a firm view on what would have happened." I asked him about the report's conclusion that lower signature debit prices would have resulted in less debit transaction acceptance by merchants, contrary to the logical assumption that lower prices lead to greater usage. He replied that "I'm not making a strong argument here, except to just say if all those things happen as I have argued, you could easily have reduced acceptance."

Dean Schmalensee's report said that it was a "fact" that lower-priced debit transactions untied from credit card transactions would have resulted in higher credit card prices. When asked what evidence supported this "fact," Schmalensee admitted that "fact is probably not the best choice of words." When I pressed Schmalensee about his statement that if credit and debit were untied, credit card prices would have been higher, he admitted, "While I think it is likely that credit card interchange fees would have risen, I haven't pushed it far enough to have an opinion." An "opinion" is what an expert testifies about, in contrast to a lay witness, who testifies about facts.

From there, it was all downhill. The defendants and the Schmalensee report said Professor Carlton should be disqualified because he had failed to account for all the additional sales that stores got when they accepted Visa/MasterCard debit transactions, citing a 5 percent "incremental" sales figure. At the deposition, Schmalensee admitted that the 5 percent figure was just made up and that he knew of nothing to support the defendants' assertion that debit cards, as contrasted with credit cards, create additional ("incremental") sales. Schmalensee testified:

> "I don't recall having seen anything from Visa that bears on that question. Certainly, I don't believe there is anything cited in here. I don't recall having seen anything else from Visa that bears on that question. No."

Schmalensee testified that he hadn't asked Visa about this key assertion in his report because "[f]or purposes of this analysis, it didn't seem particularly important."

Professor Carlton's report compared the U.S. to Canada, where effectively there was no tying arrangement between Visa/MasterCard credit and signature debit. In Canada, merchants paid no interchange fee for debit transactions, and the per-capita use of debit was more than double that in the U.S. Although Visa/MasterCard argued that the Canadian comparison was irrelevant, Schmalensee testified that "what went on in Canada might be a very interesting case study. I haven't done it."

Finally, because we had the Schmalensee report filed in the *Microsoft* case, we pointed out to Judge Gleeson that Schmalensee's position on tying arrangements in that case was contrary to the position that Visa/MasterCard were taking in the Merchants' case. In *Microsoft*, Dean Schmalensee said that forcing personal computer manufacturers, who used the Windows operating system, to install Microsoft's Internet Explorer web browser was not a tying arrangement, because Microsoft did not charge anything extra for the browser.

In the Merchants' case, Heller Ehrman asserted that a tying arrangement could harm competition only if the second "tied" product were provided without extra charge. Heller Ehrman was contradicting Dean Schmalensee, its own expert, in a position he had taken during the exact same time period in *Microsoft*, the most publicized antitrust case in history. Heller Ehrman also seemed to be attempting to harmonize the positions it was asserting for yet another client, the 3M Corporation, in yet another case, *LePage v. 3M*.

Over the years, I have taken or defended the depositions of many of the leading industrial organization economists in antitrust cases. Admissions like those made during Dean Schmalensee's deposition are rare. Just one can seriously erode the credibility and usefulness of an expert for that case. Dean Schmalensee made more than a dozen such admissions at his two-day deposition. While he was doing this and answering my long and complex questions about hypothetical situations, his lawyer from Heller Ehrman sat virtually silent. His first objection to a question came on page 176 of the deposition transcript, during the second day. It seemed to me that the Heller Ehrman lawyer was implicitly saying, "I am not afraid of anything you ask him." Schmalensee was therefore left to defend himself. I believe that because he was already fully booked on *Microsoft*, Schmalensee was pressured to act as Visa/MasterCard's expert on the class motion. To his credit, Dean Schmalansee would not dissemble while under oath. He admitted to the minimal amount of work he had done and constantly refused to endorse a position in "his" report that he couldn't agree with or hadn't studied.

As we left Dean Schmalensee's deposition, we were confident that the effort to disqualify Professor Carlton and defeat our class motion would fail. Judge Gleeson's subsequent decision confirmed our beliefs. His decision referred to many of Schmalensee's admissions, highlighting his confession that he hadn't actually formed an "opinion" on the defendants' primary basis for seeking to disqualify Professor Carlton. Judge Gleeson also pointed out that if he were to accept Visa/MasterCard's argument about why Carlton should be disqualified, he would disqualify Schmalansee. But, of course, Judge

Gleeson didn't have to disqualify Schmalensee. Dean Schmalensee was relieved of his duties in the Merchants' case after his deposition. He had already filed a preliminary report on the merits of the case, but Visa's final expert report on that subject was eventually authored by a replacement, Dr. Ben Klein.

The Schmalensee report and deposition showed me that the defendants were not merely vulnerable, but beginning to crumble. This impression deepened after another incident in the Carlton/ Schmalensee expert witness duel. This incident began while I was defending Professor Carlton's deposition in Chicago and involved the seemingly minor issue of whether Heller Ehrman would depose Carlton for one or two days. Magistrate Judge Mann had already rejected our proposal to limit the number of depositions but did adopt a two-day limit for each deposition, instead of our one-day proposal. Both sides assumed that this two-day limit would not apply to experts. However, leaving nothing to chance, when it came time to depose Dr. Carlton about his class motion report, the parties asked the magistrate judge to rule on whether this two-day limit applied to experts. On May 25, 1999, during the first hour of Carlton's deposition in Chicago, we were interrupted and handed a copy of Mann's decision limiting the time Carlton could be deposed to two days.

I called for a break in Carlton's deposition, which I was defending. Carlton was being deposed by Steve Bomse, a famous and distinguished antitrust lawyer at Heller Ehrman. I asked Bomse whether he would question Carlton for one day and reserve the second day for later, or immediately use both days. When Bomse said he would use both days right then, I warned him that Carlton would submit a second supplementary report supporting the class motion. I suggested to Bomse that he might want to depose Carlton for one day on the first report and reserve the second day for Carlton's supplementary report.

He rejected this suggestion and resumed the deposition, which continued for two full days.

Eighteen months later, in Heller Ehrman's brief to the United States Court of Appeals for the Second Circuit seeking to overturn Judge Gleeson's certification of the class, there was a footnote arguing how unfair it was that they had been unable to depose Professor Carlton after his second report. It was asserted that this had deprived the defendants of the opportunity to subject Carlton's additional findings to cross-examination under oath. I assumed that Heller Ehrman associates had written the brief without knowing what had happened, and that Bomse had not spotted the false assertion when he reviewed the brief. So, I called Bomse and left him a voice mail message about the misrepresentation and gave him the opportunity to file a corrected version of the brief. Bomse responded with a voice mail message of his own, which I had transcribed. He said:

> **"...I am not gonna hide behind the notion that I didn't know about what was in the brief, and I certainly am not going to suggest to you that I have forgotten agreements that in fact were made and you have recited with precision. Having said that, I will stand entirely by the footnote."**

Bomse justified his position by complaining about how much of Dr. Carlton's analysis was contained in the second report. He did this despite admitting that I had given him the opportunity to depose Carlton after we filed the second report, and also admitting that he had declined the offer. Steve Bomse is a famous antitrust lawyer, a straight shooter and a man I like and look up to. To me, his refusal to change that footnote was a sign that as the stakes mounted, Heller Ehrman was beginning to panic. As the reader will soon see, this particular sign of panic intensified and dramatically played out in open court months later.

On February 22, 2000, 18 days after oral argument of the class action motion, in the United States District Court in Brooklyn, Judge Gleeson granted class certification in a 45-page opinion. If the class action doctrine, codified in Rule 23 of the Federal Rules of Civil Procedure, had been applied by the blindfolded goddess in the way we are taught by our 11th-grade social studies teachers that justice is meted out, Judge Gleeson's opinion need not have been 45 pages. The decision could have been 4.5 pages or just these 45 words, which Judge Gleeson wrote and, 20 months later, the United States Court of Appeals repeated:

> **"This is precisely the type of situation for which the class action device is suited...without class certification, there are likely to be numerous motions to intervene and millions of small merchants will lose any practical means of obtaining damages for defendants' allegedly illegal conduct."**

That was the simple truth. The case was enormously complicated and difficult, but the class issue should have been a no-brainer. The above judicial statement recognized this, in the midst of a long and unnecessarily complicated analysis. Millions of stores were in the class. These stores were all challenging the exact same Visa/Master-Card conduct and identical tying arrangements. The tying arrangements were part of the contracts used by every one of the thousands of Visa/MasterCard banks. It was not merely "impracticable," as Rule 23 requires, but impossible for the vast majority of the five million stores to bring separate lawsuits against Visa/MasterCard. Had even one percent done so, this would have choked the federal courts with 50,000 lawsuits.

Recognizing the simplicity of the class determination, while giving this massive case its due, Gleeson wrote 43 pages of well-reasoned opinion. However, on page 44, Judge Gleeson apparently lost his nerve. He said that the class certification raised "substantial and novel questions" and asked the Second Circuit to review his decision, under a new provision of Rule 23 of the Federal Rules of Civil Procedure. This new rule permitted a circuit court to hear an immediate appeal of a class-certification decision. Begging a higher court to give a losing party the opportunity to attack one's ruling is a rare and odd step for a confident jurist.

There are several possible explanations for why Judge Gleeson did this. He may really have believed that our case raised novel issues. If so, he was wrong. Anyone can characterize the issues in a case so as to distinguish them from every previous case. However, in our case these distinctions made no difference that was meaningful to the law. When Case B involves the identical legal principle previously established in Case A, the party seeking to avoid the precedent established in Case A may argue that Case A involved conduct on Tuesday, whereas the conduct in Case B occurred on Wednesday. A judge should quickly reject that argument. Judge Gleeson rejected, but then characterized as "novel," distinctions as irrelevant as Tuesday versus Wednesday.

A second possible explanation for Judge Gleeson's self-doubt involves his possible reluctance to be the judge to certify the class leading to a huge, even record, damage award. Judge Gleeson, like me, is ambitious. I believe that he wants to be appointed to the bench of the Second Circuit, and perhaps his aspirations go even higher. Presiding over and facilitating the payment by banks of billions of dollars to a class led by Wal-Mart was not the best route to judicial promotion at that moment. The *Wall Street Journal* regularly bashes trial lawyers and "judicial activists" for creating monstrous awards and settlements in class actions. These articles and editorials come from the folks who hang out at the Cato Institute, the Heritage Foundation, the American Enterprise Institute, and, especially, the Federalist Society. They are among the people whom Ronald Reagan and, later, George W. Bush, packed the courts with.

Instead of stepping up to the plate and unequivocally certifying the no-brainer class, Judge Gleeson seemed to want to protect his flank, if not cover his ass. His equivocating plea to the Second Circuit to look over his shoulder and grade his work product made it virtually certain that the Court of Appeals would grant this discretionary appeal. Without Judge Gleeson's request, the appeal would not likely have been accepted, because the circuit courts treat such requests (for immediate review of a decision on class certification) like the Supreme Court treats a petition for certiorari: They rarely are granted.

Because Judge Gleeson asked it to, the Second Circuit granted Visa/MasterCard's request and agreed to hear their appeal. The Court of Appeals then allowed the process to advance as slowly as possible. When Visa/MasterCard made their request for an immediate appeal to the Second Circuit on March 8, 2000, that court hadn't even bothered to establish any rules or procedures for dealing with such a petition or for expediting the process, as we requested. Knowing that Judge Gleeson's plea for review made acceptance of the defendants' appeal a forgone conclusion, we had requested an expedited decision on the defendants' petition. This was our desperate effort to maintain the trial date of November 27, 2000, which Judge Gleeson had established in his scheduling order issued on December 20, 1999. Expedited appeals are supposed to proceed quickly. Making up their new procedure as they went along, the Second Circuit granted our motion to "expedite" on April 5, 2000. However, under this so-called expedited procedure, the court didn't actually hear the appeal until February 5, 2001, and didn't decide it until October 17, 2001.

This glacial schedule obviously killed the November 27, 2000 trial date. Seemingly oblivious to the advisory accompanying the new appeals provision, which said that such appeals *"should not delay existing cases,"* the Court of Appeals, over our objection, granted Visa/MasterCard an extended schedule for filing their appellate briefs. Again, despite our objection, the court also agreed to Visa's request that the appeal not be argued during certain periods when Larry Popofsky, Visa's lead lawyer, was scheduled to be in Europe. The circuit court then had difficulty assembling a panel to hear the appeal and rescinded the initial order scheduling an argument in 2000. The court rescheduled the argument for February 5, 2001, nearly a full year after Judge Gleeson's decision certifying the class. Again, all of this was done by the Second Circuit under an appeals procedure that the Supreme Court of the United States had designed "not to delay existing cases."

The panel that was finally assembled to hear the appeal comprised Circuit Judge Sonia Sotomayor, District Court Judge Denise Cote, sitting in the Second Circuit by "designation," and Circuit Judge Dennis Jacobs. Judge Jacobs is a founder of the Federalist Society, a powerful organization that promotes the constitutional and legal agenda of the American right wing. For cases not falling into the Federalist Society's hit list, Judge Jacobs is a fine and open-minded jurist. But when you go before him with a case presenting an issue on the neo-conservative agenda, Judge Jacobs's vote is virtually a forgone conclusion. So, I assumed that we were starting out with one vote on the panel against us, because our case was the biggest ever example of one of the great *bêtes noires* of American neo-conservatism, "the class action."

A book can be written about why neo-cons hate class actions, with lots of liberal assertions and rejoinders from the right. And while class actions, like all legal mechanisms, can be abused and sometimes are, the simple truth is that class actions, in many situations, give little guys their only real ability to receive justice and compensation. That is precisely what both Judge Gleeson and a majority of the Second Circuit said was true in the Merchants' case, involving five million mostly small stores. That is why the American right hated the Merchants' case.

With less confidence than our prediction about Judge Jacobs, we counted Judge Sotomayor as a likely vote to affirm the class certification order. Our confidence was based on the overwhelmingly clear and simple legal principles in our favor. Our knowledge of, and research into, Judge Sotomayor's judicial opinions showed she was a pragmatist and followed established precedent, unless there was some compelling reason to depart from it. Another factor that suggested that Judge Sotomayor would vote to affirm the class certification was her generally populist orientation. Nevertheless, our prediction on Sotomayor was less confident than with Jacobs because Judge Gleeson, in his own way a populist, had telegraphed his self-doubt by making his decision far more complicated than necessary, and by pleading for the Second Circuit to review his work. As important to me as the likelihood that Judge Jacobs would seek to reverse the class certification, and that Judge Sotomayor vote to uphold it, was whether she would actively engage him over their assumed diverging positions and fight for an ally and deciding vote in the third member of the panel, United States District Judge Denise Cote.

Denise Cote, from the Southern District of New York, was perceived by virtually everybody on both sides as the swing vote. I say "virtually" because I was mildly confident that she would vote to affirm. My prior contact with her was minimal, but I knew she was very smart, had been taught by the best, and was a good judge of men. In the mid-1970s, Denise Cote had clerked for Eastern District Judge Jack Weinstein. Weinstein was the author of the Federal Rules of Evidence, a preeminent master of federal procedure and an intellectual giant. His clerks went into his chambers among the brightest, and left having learned at the feet of one of the truly great jurists of the twentieth century. Weinstein had skillfully handled some of the most difficult class actions, including the Agent Orange, tobacco, asbestos and handgun cases.

Denise Cote had clerked for Judge Weinstein in 1976 when I had a case before him. The case required me to argue before a "three-judge constitutional court," an arcane procedure used back then, involving a mixed panel of circuit court and district court judges to hear challenges to the constitutionality of state laws. After the hearing, Denise came out to express Judge Weinstein's praise for my "brilliant, but likely futile" argument challenging the constitutionality of a New York welfare statute that discriminated against the working poor. The three judges were Weinstein, Circuit Judge Tom Meskill (the former governor of Connecticut) and District Judge Mark Cosentino, a judge annually ranked among the "10 Worst" by lefty columnist Jack Newfield of the *Village Voice*.

Judge Weinstein or Cote, or likely both, wrote a 46-page dissent from the majority opinion, which Weinstein later told me had been written to reward my "Quixotic effort." Denise Cote paid me an even higher compliment by sending a message, through an intermediary, that I should ask her out on a date. Through the same go-between, I truthfully responded that I thought she was very attractive and would ask her out in my "next life," because I had recently gotten married. It was the smarts and the Weinstein tutelage on class actions, more than the ancient spark, which I was sure she had forgotten, that gave me confidence in Denise Cote's vote.

Others thought that Judge Cote could go either way. She had spent part of her career doing antitrust work at the Kaye Scholer law firm. That firm was almost always on the defense side. Mark Popofsky, who was a Kaye Scholer partner and the son of Visa's lead lawyer Larry Popofsky, sent an e-mail to every lawyer at Kaye Scholer asking for information about Judge Cote so Visa might shape its argument to her liking, or at least sharpen the prediction of her vote. When I found out about this poll, I was amused, except for one moment of fear. I was scared that Cote might have been at Kaye Scholer in 1989 and involved in their representation of MasterCard at the time of the Rusty Staub's incident. I feared that she might recuse herself, requiring that she be replaced on the appeals court panel. That didn't happen.

On the evening of February 4, 2001, the night before my oral argument of the class certification appeal in the Second Circuit, I checked into a hotel near the courthouse. This has always been custom when I have a very important argument. I checked into the Millenium Hotel in downtown Manhattan, where certain rooms have a view of the majestic United States Courthouse in Foley Square, home to the United States Court of Appeals for the Second Circuit. My view that night was not of the courthouse but of the World Trade Center, where I had worked for seven years. The Twin Towers were directly in front of me—so close, I felt, that I could have touched them. I stared at the Trade Center for a long time that night as I rehearsed my argument in the dark of my hotel room. That is my last and abiding image of the World Trade Center.

On the next day, February 5, 2001, oral argument was well presented by both sides. The defendants made one tactical error, and I made one as well. Visa/MasterCard's error was to divide their argument. It is usually a mistake to divide the short amount of time allotted for oral argument of an appeal. Unless perfectly choreographed, divided argument tends to be disjointed and requires the court to readjust to a new speaker and new salutations. They get to hear "May it please the Court, my name is Joe Blow" for the second time right in the middle of those precious few minutes. Because advocates are constantly responding to questions from the bench, appellate argument rarely permits the perfect choreography necessary to make a mid-argument baton pass work well. Visa and MasterCard may have divided their argument to symbolically rebut our claim that they jointly fronted for the same bank cartel, or it might have been a matter of professional pride among the defendants. However, because Visa and MasterCard filed a single brief, dividing argument was a tactical error, and it led to an actual error during the argument.

Visa had convinced the Second Circuit to black out certain dates to ensure that Larry Popofsky could make his trips to Europe and still argue the case. However, after all that and the months of delay it caused, Steve Bomse argued the appeal for Visa. MasterCard, apparently convinced that their previous lead lawyers at Clifford Chance had performed badly, inserted Ken Gallo to argue. Substituting Gallo as lead counsel was a smart move. During the previous summer of 2000, the rugged "alpha-male" had proved himself to be the best trial lawyer in the United States trial against Visa/MasterCard. I had witnessed much of the trial and was struck by the extra attention Judge Barbara Jones seemed to give Gallo's "directs" and cross-examinations. However, using a crucial Second Circuit argument as Gallo's first appearance in our case was foolish. He was coming in after the conclusion of all fact discovery and after all of the expert reports and depositions had been completed. He hadn't been part of the class proceedings and didn't yet know the case. Toward the end of his argument, he gave an answer to a pointed question that exposed his unfamiliarity with the record.

In his oral argument, Gallo mounted an attack on Professor Carlton's supplementary expert report. Judge Cote interrupted and pointedly asked Gallo why the defendants hadn't deposed Professor Carlton after this second report. Cote was seemingly challenging

Gallo on defendants' misrepresentation, which I had exposed with very specific documentation in our brief.

> JUDGE COTE: "If it was so flawed, that is, his second affidavit, why did you decline to take his deposition?"

Gallo clearly knew nothing about this, and his answer showed it.

> GALLO: "...we made a tactical decision that we could not take his deposition. It was outside of the period allowed for expert discovery. There was a period, and then the deposition period had ended at that point, is my recollection of the record."

To the panel, it probably seemed like the defendants were compounding the blatant misrepresentation in the footnote I had earlier requested of Steve Bomse that he correct. Dissatisfaction with Gallo's response was reflected in the faces of all three judges, who probably wondered whether Gallo was lying or clueless. As I was watching this play out, so was Steve Bomse, whose time for argument had expired. Nevertheless, when Gallo finished, Bomse jumped up, realizing that it was a big mistake to allow the appellate court's last impression of Visa/MasterCard to be one of bumblers or liars.

> BOMSE: "May I ask for the Court's indulgence, just to respond to the factual question that Judge Cote put to Mr. Gallo that he would not have known the answer to, but that I do."
>
> JUDGE JACOBS: "Yes, if you can do that very briefly."
>
> BOMSE: "Yes. Why we didn't take a deposition after the reply. The answer was that we were told—we had, two days in which to take the deposition, and we used those two days going to the

opening declaration, therefore, we had no right or no ability to take that deposition."

Although Bomse had now partially come clean, he hadn't completely, by saying Visa/MasterCard had "no ability." Bomse certainly hadn't admitted the blatant misrepresentation in the defendants' appellate brief. So, I improperly jumped up to correct the record.

CONSTANTINE: "Your Honor, I looked at Mr. Bomse on May 25th, 1999 and I said, 'We are going to file a reply declaration. Would you like to take a day of deposition now and a day after the reply?' And Mr. Bomse, and he will obviously admit that, indicated that he would take his full two days then. Thank you."

These kinds of impromptu hijinks are not supposed to occur in the second most prestigious courtroom in our nation. However, my improvised part in this "Keystone Cops" scene was not my tactical error during the argument. Mine was to bother with Judge Jacobs at all. Among the three judges on the panel, I'd decided to focus my argument squarely on him. I attempted to appeal to his better nature and directly confront his well-known neo-conservative tendencies. At the beginning of my argument, I turned directly to Judge Jacobs and argued that he and everybody else knew that there really was no serious doubt about the propriety of certifying this class, and that the only reason that the circuit court was hearing the appeal was because so much money was potentially at stake. Although the principle or issue of law should govern the outcome of a case, not the amount of money involved, I said, "Let's talk about that.... We are here because of the big number involved in this case. So the question is, what do you do with that?"

Jacobs nodded his agreement with my point that the only reason

Judge Gleeson had asked the Second Circuit to take the case, and the only reason they had, was "the enormous financial consequences [for the defendants] of class certification." And I quoted for Judge Jacobs the famous observation of Supreme Court Justice Oliver Wendell Holmes that "great cases make bad law because they are deemed great because of some immediate overwhelming interest which distorts judgment, making what previously seemed clear to seem doubtful." And then building upon Justice Holmes, I told Jacobs:

> **"The immediate overwhelming interest in this case is the amount of money claimed…by the plaintiffs against the defendants. That is what is really going on in this case."**

Judge Jacobs again nodded his agreement with my statement. Confronting this issue head-on was not an effective tactic with Judge Jacobs, a man on a mission to torpedo class actions in general, and especially this one, which I impertinently reminded him was perhaps the biggest in federal court history.

Judge Jacobs's dissenting opinion was a tirade against class actions, class action lawyers and how honest folk like Visa/Master-Card were being judicially blackmailed into settling frivolous class actions. Judge Jacobs's opinion contained virtually every right-wing ideological cliché about class actions and plaintiffs' lawyers. While Jacobs denied any view on the ultimate merits of the case, he disclosed uncertainty concerning the legal issues actually presented. Early in his dissent, Jacobs observed:

> **"Even a defendant who is innocent and holy may rationally choose to pay a few hundred million dollars in settlement of a class rather than 'run the risk of ruinous liability.'"**

Was Jacobs's assessment that Visa/MasterCard were "innocent and holy?" Perhaps not. Maybe this was Jacobs's advice to Visa/MasterCard on the proper settlement amount, if indeed they were innocent. Judge Jacobs sarcastically said that "if each merchant's claim took no more than half a day to sort out, the damages phase of trial would last as long as the whole course of Western Civilization from Ur." However, the scientific advances of Eastern and Western civilization, namely the invention of the abacus and the digital computer, would make calculation of damages for five million class members simple and straightforward under our damages formula.

Judge Jacobs actually suggested that the stores were eager accomplices in their own injuries, expecting that the money they lost would be returned threefold because antitrust damages are automatically tripled, Judge Jacobs stated: "An antitrust plaintiff seeking treble damages can profit by avoiding mitigation of loss." Finally, Jacobs took a cheap shot at me by saying that plaintiffs' counsel had improperly "herded together" dissimilar stores into a class to their detriment, in a quest for attorneys' fees. Jacobs contended that my herding of dissimilar claims together in this class demonstrated the inadequacy of my representation. However, this ground was not asserted by the defendants, as Judge Sotomayor pointed out, in her October 17, 2001, majority opinion joined by Judge Cote, upholding the class certification. Therefore, Judge Sotomayor demonstrated, it was not a proper ground for reversal. Such appellate rules and the clear principles of law applied by Judge Sotomayor in the majority opinion don't govern judges with a predetermined agenda.

The launching pad for all of these counterfactual discussions was Judge Jacobs's assumption that when the defendants forced stores to pay higher prices for debit transactions, they lowered the price charged for credit transactions. Jacobs had to avoid both the facts and the law to do this. He avoided the law, which said that Judge

Gleeson's finding that credit card rates wouldn't have declined could only be disregarded if Jacobs found that Gleeson's factual determination was "clearly erroneous." Judge Jacobs didn't make that finding because he couldn't. He couldn't, because all of the evidence in the record went in the other direction. The evidence showed that as important as it was to Visa/MasterCard to gouge the stores on debit prices, to destroy the regional debit networks and to monopolize the debit market, it was equally or more important for defendants to maintain their credit card monopoly. Judge Jacobs couldn't rebut the evidence in the record about this, such as a Visa document that measured the value of suppressing the regional debit networks. The record showed that the defendants' conduct caused an escalation in Visa/MasterCard credit card prices of hundreds of millions of dollars.

Because Judge Jacobs could not rebut this evidence, because there was nothing in the record for him to use, he just ignored it. His dissent was written in a manner sure to get the attention of Justice Antonin Scalia, the leading neo-conservative Supreme Court Justice at the time. Justice Scalia, like Judge Jacobs, is a founder of the Federalist Society (where I have been a guest speaker). The dissent gave Visa/MasterCard their only chance of getting the Supreme Court to hear their appeal of the Second Circuit's decision. Visa and MasterCard made this request by filing a petition for certiorari.

The petition for certiorari, which extensively quoted Judge Jacobs's dissent, was designed to attract the attention of Justice Scalia, Justice Clarence Thomas and the late Chief Justice William Rehnquist. Nevertheless, the petition still had little chance of success and was primarily used as another delaying tactic by Visa/MasterCard. The delay game was the one the defendants consistently won throughout the case. The courts were extraordinarily accommodating to the defendants' desire to stall. First, Magistrate Judge Mann, then the Second Circuit, then Judge Gleeson and, finally, the Supreme Court.

By filing and losing a motion to reargue the appeal in the Second Circuit, the defendants stopped the 90-day clock on their time to file a petition for certiorari in the Supreme Court. After this, the defendants had until March 4, 2002, to file their "cert." petition. Our opposition to the petition would have been due no later than April 3, 2002, making virtually certain that the Supreme Court would decide the petition before the Court adjourned in June. The summer recess lasts until the first week in October. Delaying the petition for certiorari could extend the delay by four months from June to October. This is how the defendants tried, and almost succeeded, in getting this additional delay.

The defendants hired yet another big law firm, Sidley & Austin, and Sidley's well-known Supreme Court specialist, Carter Philips. Philips made a motion to extend the time to file defendants' petition for certiorari from March 4, 2002, until April 3, 2002. Philips's request for the delay argued that he was too busy working on other Supreme Court cases to file a timely petition for Visa and MasterCard. To make sure that we had no opportunity to oppose this motion, the defendants' papers were sent to us by regular mail on the same day that the motion was delivered to Supreme Court Justice Ruth Bader Ginsburg. Prior to this, the parties had served each other with motion papers on the same day they were filed in court, by using hand delivery, fax, or overnight service. Regular mail from Washington to New York City is normally slow, but in March 2002 it was even slower. Such mail was coming from and going to the two cities that had recently experienced anthrax attacks on their post offices. C&P received the defendants' request for an extension nine days after it was mailed to us, and six days after Justice Ginsburg granted Visa and MasterCard an extension of their time to file a cert. petition.

We consulted a Supreme Court specialist at a firm we were

friendly with. We also consulted former U.S. Solicitor General Barbara Underwood. They both told us that the extension would likely delay the Court's decision on whether to hear Visa/MasterCard's appeal until October 2002 instead of June. Attempting to avoid this, we tried to anticipate the defendants' arguments and wrote most of our response to the defendants' petition for certiorari before we received it. Our predictions about the arguments Visa and Master-Card would make in their petition were good. We were able to file our opposition 11 days early. A clerk in the Supreme Court, aware of the game-playing by the defendants, complimented us on our quick response. He observed that "rarely, if ever, are opposition papers filed as early as yours were filed in this case."

The defendants' petition for certiorari was not compelling. The primary reason that the Supreme Court will grant a petition for certiorari and hear an appeal is because the case raises some important and novel issue and/or because the Court of Appeals has decided the case in a way that conflicts with an important ruling of another Court of Appeals in another "Circuit." Neither factor was present in our case. The defendants' petition advanced bogus novel issues and nonexistent conflicts, but not very convincingly.

More impressive than the arguments advanced in the defendants' cert. petition were the names, number and size of the organizations that filed *amicus curiae* or "friend of the court" briefs urging the Supreme Court to grant the defendants' petition. Visa/Master-Card's friends included the Alliance of Automobile Manufacturers, the American Chemistry Council, the American Council of Life Insurers, the American Insurance Association, the American Petroleum Institute, the Association of American Railroads, the California Bankers Association, the European-American Business Council, the Institute of International Bankers, the Mortgage Bankers Association of America, the Pharmaceutical Research and Manufacturers of America, the Texas Bankers Association, the American Bankers Association, the Consumer Bankers Association, the Financial Services Roundtable, the Independent Community Bankers of America, America's Community Bankers, the Delaware Bankers Association, the New Mexico Bankers Association, the New York Bankers Association, the New York Clearing House Association, the North Carolina Bankers Association, the Oklahoma Bankers Association, the South Carolina Bankers Association and the Fertilizer Institute. I frequently point out that Visa/MasterCard was a front for a bank cartel. As the above list shows, the cartel showed up in force for this event. In supporting Visa/MasterCard, these friends were represented by three additional law firms and Drew Days, a former United States Solicitor General.

Uncomfortably close to adjourning for the summer, the Supreme Court, without dissent, denied defendants' petition for certiorari on June 10, 2002. Though it had eaten up much more time than we desired, taking 39 months from start to finish, another crucial battle had been won. The case had been certified as a class action on behalf of five million merchants by the district court and confirmed by the Court of Appeals. The Supreme Court had declined to review this result. Judge Gleeson ordered us to appear back in court 11 days later, on June 21, 2002, and rescheduled the trial for April 28, 2003.

At the same June 21 conference, Judge Gleeson granted a motion made months before by the *Wall Street Journal* to unseal most of the documents hidden from the public in the sealed court file. However, before the documents in the court file could be unsealed, they actually had to be in the court file. Many of them weren't there, and many of the rest were misfiled. Realizing this, Magistrate Judge Mann called for our help. A team of lawyers and paralegals from C&P, led by Amy Roth, went in and restored the file to order so it could be unsealed. After these documents were unsealed, examined and excerpted in the

Wall Street Journal, the *New York Times* and scores of other papers, the observation in Judge Jacobs's dissent about "innocent and holy" defendants who are coerced to settle class actions could no longer be used to describe Visa/MasterCard.

Unsealing the Shark

———

OVER THE COURSE of the first five years of the litigation, the press interest in the Merchants' case steadily increased, especially in business periodicals such as *Fortune, Forbes, Business Week*, the *Financial Times* and the *Wall Street Journal*. The case was vilified on the *Journal*'s editorial pages but conspicuously and fairly reported in that paper's news section, many times on the front page. One *Journal* reporter, John Wilke, sensed that the case would be historic and that the largely sealed discovery file contained many documents that Visa, MasterCard and the banks never wanted to see the light of day. Wilke asked Stuart Karle, the *Journal*'s General Counsel, to file a motion asking Judge Gleeson to unseal the court file. Unsealing would permit the public to find out what was really happening in a case that involved virtually all of America's stores and consumers. The *Journal*'s motion to unseal, which later was joined by other newspapers, was granted by Judge Gleeson at the June 21, 2002, court hearing.

The articles that appeared in the *Wall Street Journal*, the *New York Times* and scores of other papers, after Judge Gleeson unsealed the file, cast the defendants and their case in a very bad light. These articles, first published on November 14, 2002, analyzed unsealed

Visa/MasterCard documents showing, among other things, that in 1988 Visa had asked MasterCard to remove the markings on debit cards that allowed merchants and consumers to distinguish debit cards from credit cards, and that MasterCard had agreed to this request. The *Times* quoted unsealed portions of the deposition testimony of Edward Hogan, a MasterCard executive, about the Visa/MasterCard meeting where the agreement to remove the markings had occurred.

The *Journal* and *Times* also reported evidence showing how Visa and MasterCard had deceived merchants about the identity of their cards and, as the *Journal* wrote, "exploit[ed] widespread customer confusion about their branded debit cards." Electronic identifications embedded in the cards were scrambled to prevent merchants from identifying the type of Visa/MasterCard plastic card being used, as the *Journal* reported. The *Times* spotlighted MasterCard documents showing that MasterCard knew that 72 to 78 percent of cardholders confused MasterCard debit cards with MasterCard credit cards.

Other articles focused on Visa documents declaring "war" on the competing regional debit networks; documents discussing a plan to "block or disrupt formation of super-regional networks that may undercut Visa's brand dominance"; a Visa plan to "restrict deployment of PIN pads [in stores] until regionals are gone"; "'stealth' efforts by Visa to get banks to drop rival regional-network cards" and a $30 million payment from Visa to the Bank of America as part of the plot to destroy the competing regional debit networks. The *New York Times* also quoted from one of my favorite documents, a 1991 Visa memo recording what was described as "Wes' vote." This was a vote taken by Visa executive Wesley Tallman among bankers attending a Visa meeting to "wait and be sued" over the tying arrangement rather than change the practice. When Judge Gleeson unsealed the "Wes' Vote" document, he also unsealed the videotaped testimony about this vote, which I extracted from Tallman when I deposed him in San Francisco.

The *Wall Street Journal*, *New York Times* and *Associated Press* articles were then picked up by hundreds of other media outlets in the week following the November 14 press coverage. I don't believe it was coincidental that on November 20, 2002, just six days after these press reports first appeared, Magistrate Judge Mann issued a 21-page decision rejecting Visa's claim of privilege and unsealing a pivotal 50-page document. This single document was almost as damaging to the defendants' case as the thousands of documents unsealed by Judge Gleeson's order issued five months earlier. In the decision, the magistrate judge ruled that a key Visa document was not privileged and had not been mistakenly produced to us in the discovery process by Heller Ehrman, as Visa contended. Magistrate Judge Mann alternatively ruled that even if the document was privileged, that privilege had been forfeited through Heller Ehrman's negligence. I believe that the magistrate judge's timing, if not the substance of her ruling, was influenced by the November 14th press reports about the Visa/MasterCard unsealed documents. The motion to unseal this additional document had been sitting on her desk for almost two and one-half years. Although the motion had been argued by my partner Matt Cantor in August 2000, Magistrate Judge Mann issued her decision on November 20, 2002.

Judges read newspapers. The fact that some of the worst Visa/MasterCard conduct had been revealed to everyone reading these *Journal* and *Times* articles changed the case from a banks versus merchants dispute in a courthouse into a matter of general knowledge. Moreover, these and other newspapers summarized, highlighted and accented the most venal Visa/MasterCard conduct. Magistrate Judge Mann's decision followed less than a week after these conspicuous newspaper articles first appeared.

The document that the Magistrate Judge unsealed had been prepared by Andersen Consulting (now known as Accenture) for Visa in December 1997, a little more than a year after the merchants sued Visa/MasterCard and a little less than a year before the United States sued them. The document bore no title but had the names Visa and Andersen Consulting on the cover. Also on the cover were six cartoonish pictures in a style suitable for hanging in a kindergarten classroom. One was of a lower case letter "i," one of three horses, one of children's letter blocks, one of a diamond shape within a square, one of fingers "walking" across a surface and one of a smiling shark with its teeth bared. At C&P, the untitled document was called "The Shark." The transcript of the summary judgment argument of January 10, 2003, reflects me asking Jason Lipton, our paralegal, to "put The Shark up" on a huge video screen for Judge Gleeson and the packed courtroom to see. The Shark asked and answered two basic questions about our case. First, how had the tying arrangement helped Visa suppress competition? Second, what would happen if Visa were to lose the Merchants' case and be required to stop tying debit to credit and stop forcing merchants to accept Visa debit transactions?

Andersen Consulting, then a division of Arthur Andersen, had worked with Visa on its debit card strategy for more than two decades. Various witnesses described Andersen's role in Visa's debit program as being Visa's "arms and legs." The infamy of Andersen's name (fresh from its starring role in the Enron scandal) and its long and intimate connection to Visa's debit strategy raised more than a few eyebrows at the mock trials we conducted in 2003. The Shark showed that Andersen was asked two questions by Visa General Counsel, Paul Allen. First, what would happen if Visa lost the Merchants' case; and second, what the tying arrangement between debit and credit meant for Visa's business. We viewed Paul Allen (not to be confused with the President of Microsoft, who was having his own antitrust problems at the time) as Visa's Darth Vader. His dour demeanor contrasted with the otherwise sunny and upbeat Visa persona. Many legal plots and strategies that we had uncovered had been traced to Allen. At one point in the litigation, the parties had agreed to exempt from deposition a total of just three executives from both sides. Each party had an opportunity to "hide" the executive whose deposition could create the most damaging testimony. With its one selection, Visa protected Paul Allen, not Carl Pascarella, its CEO. Visa clearly feared the prospect of me deposing Allen.

After the settlement, Mr. Allen and Visa quickly parted ways. At dinner one night, Pascarella ran into Phil Bronstein, the editor of the *San Francisco Chronicle*, and Eve Burton, the General Counsel of Hearst, which owns the *Chronicle*. When Pascarella told them that Visa was looking for a new GC to replace Paul Allen, Burton asked, "What about Lloyd Constantine?" Pascarella almost lost his dinner.

In 1997, Andersen's Shark responded to Paul Allen's questions about what the tying arrangement meant to Visa by saying that the Honor All Cards tying arrangement was "a fundamental tenet of the Visa association" and "a cornerstone to the success of Visa" that had given Visa "a major competitive advantage," erected a "significant entry barrier for new players," and created the "ability of members to leverage strong Visa brand equity for all member Visa products." These answers, unfortunately for Visa and MasterCard, were not only the truth but contained many powerful buzzwords in antitrust law. Specifically, the references to "competitive advantage," "entry barrier," and allowing Visa to "leverage" power from the credit market into the debit market were the touchstones of an illegal tying arrangement.

After setting out the anticompetitive advantages of Visa's conduct, Andersen's Shark pointed out the predicament that Visa would face if the merchants were to win the case and the tying arrangement were prohibited. The Shark said that "Merchants will be able to choose which card products to accept and may potentially refuse Visa's current debit (and commercial) products." Here, Andersen dared to consider a world in which Visa's customers actually had a choice.

The Shark said that without the tying arrangement, competition would increase as it "strengthens relative position of regional network[s] in online environment." He (for some reason, I assumed The Shark was a guy) also said that ending the tying arrangement would "increase pressure on Visa to effectively end [its] ban on participation in competing national marks" including the competing American Express and Discover networks, which could not do business with Visa members under Visa By-law 2.10(e). The Shark estimated that if the tying arrangement were eliminated, Visa would lose 80 percent of its signature debit card volume and that "Visa may effectively be confined to the consumer credit market and no longer be a leader in the overall payment system market...threatening [the] overall viability of the Visa association."

Assuming Visa would lose the Merchants' case, Andersen answered Visa's question about what it would then have to do to survive. The Shark set out a range of options. The stated disadvantages of certain options were as damning to the defendants' case as the plan of action that Andersen recommended. One option was to do nothing and just leave the price of signature debit where it was. The Shark concluded that this would result in the "[r]ejection of Visa CheckCard as payment" by "merchants." This was consistent with Andersen's prediction that 80 percent of Visa's signature debit volume would be lost.

A second option was for Visa to respond by forcing the removal of competing PIN debit networks marks and functions from bank debit cards. At that time, December 1997, ATM/debit cards issued by banks usually had both the marks of networks like STAR, NYCE, Shazam and PULSE on the back and either the Visa or MasterCard mark on the front. Most still do. This permits the card to be used as either a signature debit card or a PIN debit card. Andersen envisioned a future in which merchants were no longer forced to take signature debit, but might not have the effective ability to accept the safer/faster/cheaper PIN debit because the PIN debit function had been removed from the card. When The Shark analyzed this option in December 1997, he also pointed out that there would be a threat of additional "litigation" if Visa were to take this step. This reference in the middle of the 50-page Shark speaks volumes about the tunnel vision of Visa and Andersen and the incestuous relationship of these two companies in the long and ongoing debit wars.

Although the settlement, approved by Judge Gleeson six years after this analysis was completed, prohibited Visa from pursuing this option of "mandat[ing] competing online marks off cards" (removing "STAR" etc. from the cards), Visa actually tried to remove the marks from the cards in 1998. Visa and Andersen seemed oblivious to the second and equally important Sherman Act claim in our case. The merchants claimed that Visa and MasterCard were attempting to remove competing debit marks from ATM/debit cards and thereby attempting to monopolize the debit card market. So, in the midst of the Merchants' case and into the teeth of this allegation, Visa plowed ahead. Visa used a new product that it called "Visa Checkcard II." Checkcard II, or "deuce" as it was called internally at Visa, set a price on PIN debit transactions more than five times the prevailing marketplace rate for these transactions. But for a bank to be able to charge that quintupled price to merchants, it had to remove all of the competing debit network marks from the cards. Visa gave the banks a four hundred percent price increase as a reward for destroying Visa and MasterCard's competitors. This would also force merchants to accept the higher Visa PIN debit price, because the alternative competing networks would disappear from the backs of ATM/debit cards.

C&P quickly got wind of this plan and alerted the Federal Trade Commission. The documents surrounding this Visa Checkcard II gambit were among the most damaging to Visa and played a prominent role in our summary judgment submissions. The FTC investigated and, later, so did the Antitrust Division. Visa was forced to back down from this plan a year later. However, it did so only after all this additional evidence had been created and severe damage was done to its defense in the Merchants' case. Visa did all this after being warned by The Shark that if it were to take these steps, additional litigation would likely ensue.

Making an awful situation worse, Visa even constructed a cover story. An unsealed, handwritten Visa document from 1999 stated that the real reason that Visa would capitulate and rescind the rule forcing competing debit network names and functions to be removed from the cards was because of the Department of Justice investigation and the merchants' lawsuit. However, the document also said that Visa should explain the change in policy as merely Visa reconsidering the action and deciding that it didn't make sense. The unsealed deposition testimony of Visa's CEO, Carl Pascarella, shows that when I asked him why Visa had dropped the rule, he answered with a variation of this cover story.

Andersen's Shark also recommended several other actions Visa could take if it were to lose the Merchants' case. These options were legally less risky and more realistic. One recommended option involved developing a so-called Visa "brand extension" for debit cards, meaning that in addition to the Visa name, the word "debit" or another word conveying the meaning of debit would appear on every Visa debit card. The recommendation also required Visa to lower the interchange price for signature debit transactions so that merchants, who were free to reject the transactions, would have an incentive to continue accepting them.

The Shark was crucial during the litigation because it showed Andersen telling Visa that the merchants' allegations about the predatory nature of the tying arrangements were correct. By being so specific about how the tying arrangements hurt merchants and consumers, The Shark gave Judge Gleeson a clear road map for the relief he should grant in order to protect them in the future.

The Shark also showed that our theory of how the merchants were monetarily damaged was correct. We said that without the tying arrangements, Visa/MasterCard would have had to lower their prices to maintain merchant acceptance. Visa/MasterCard told the court that this theory was absurd and that its proponents, Professors Frank Fisher and Dennis Carlton, were practicing junk science. However, The Shark agreed with Fisher and Carlton. This Andersen analysis confirmed Fisher's methodology and made it highly unlikely that the defendants would be able to get Judge Gleeson to reject our damage theory. Had Frank Fisher testified at trial, he would have pointed to The Shark as confirming his analysis.

The Shark delivered his last great gift on his last page. Andersen predicted that Visa By-law 2.10(e), the Visa rule that targeted competitors but blatantly shouted that "MasterCard is not our competitor," would be declared illegal. Coming in December 1997, this prediction occurred ten months before the United States had even filed suit to invalidate that Visa by-law and MasterCard's similar "Competitive Programs Policy." Our complaint said that Visa By-law 2.10(e) and MasterCard's CPP harmed competition in both the credit card and debit card markets. But the apparent assignment of Andersen was to analyze what would happen to Visa if the tying arrangement were invalidated. Andersen's seemingly gratuitous prediction that another Visa rule would be found illegal was likely to offend Judge Gleeson. Judge Gleeson would probably infer that Visa was enforcing a rule that it knew was illegal, that Visa knew that Gleeson would invalidate it, or that the rule would be the subject of yet another suit by the U.S., or maybe all of these. These were the logical inferences I asked Judge Gleeson to take away when I showed him The Shark and projected his image on a giant video screen during my summary judgment argument on January 10, 2003.

Double Jeopardy

———

THE CLASS CERTIFICATION contest involved more work than the entirety of many large and complex commercial cases. But that effort was dwarfed by the battle over the summary judgment motions. Summary judgment is primarily a defendant's tool in antitrust cases. The defense asks the judge to prevent some or all of the plaintiff's case from going to trial. My style of litigating, however, is to avoid, whenever possible, going into any battle where only my side has something to lose. I try to turn any contest, including summary judgment, into one involving reciprocal jeopardy. I do this unless my chances of success are inconsequential.

In this case, despite the skepticism of many lawyers on our side, I decided to put the defendants in jeopardy when they moved to throw out our case. We had uncovered so much compelling evidence during the discovery process that I believed that this was the rare antitrust case in which the judge might find for the plaintiff before trial on some of the disputed issues. If Judge Gleeson were to do this, he would instruct the jury that certain facts and issues, which we normally would have the burden to prove, were already proven. Regardless of our chance of success, I wanted the psychological and emotional lift that going on the offensive would give our team. The size of the discovery record and the ferocity of defendants' opposition to the class motion made me certain that the summary judgment proceedings would involve an enormous effort. I didn't want my team to work that hard with the only possible outcomes being that all or part of our case would be dismissed or, at best, we would stay right where we were. We needed to have something big to win and had to give the defendants something big to lose.

The hardest part of the summary judgment contest was that it came directly after, and actually overlapped, three other crucial and withering battles. These were the class motion, the final weeks of fact discovery, and the short, intense period of expert discovery. I argued the class motion on February 4, 2000. The class was certified on February 22, 2000. From February 1 through March 27, 2000, which included only 40 days when depositions could be taken, the parties took exactly 200 depositions. As soon as fact discovery ended, Judge Gleeson required the expert reports and expert depositions to be completed by April 4, 2000. During a 43-day window, 21 experts filed reports and/or rebuttal reports and were deposed for as long as four days each.

We informed Judge Gleeson that we would be moving for summary judgment when the defendants moved. We requested that the briefs for both sides be filed on the same dates, making it necessary for both sides to attack and defend simultaneously and intensifying the double jeopardy dynamic. Judge Gleeson obliged, initially requiring the opening briefs on June 2, 2000, opposition briefs on June 30, 2000, reply briefs on July 17, 2000, and oral argument on August 4, 2000. By cramming so much work into such a short period of time, Judge Gleeson was giving himself the opportunity to reduce the size of the case before trial, which was scheduled for November 27, 2000.

Each of our summary judgment briefs tried to summarize and synthesize the affidavits and evidence that accompanied our briefs and totaled more than 50,000 pages. The briefs and exhibits were our distillation of a discovery record of roughly five million pages of documents and 150,000 pages of deposition testimony. So, while it was appropriate and smart for Judge Gleeson to set this vicious schedule, it was somewhat like directing the parties to seat six elephants in a VW Beetle, by putting three in the back and three in the front.

I gave my young partner, Gordon Schnell, the job of being our elephant installer. Gordon is a diminutive, quiet, reserved and extremely affable lawyer. He does not look like a player in the blood sport of complex commercial litigation. However, as a kid, Gordon had been New Jersey's 60-pound scholastic wrestling champion. Anyone who has watched a match involving middle-school and high-school wrestlers in the miniature weight categories knows their tenacity. As a decent, but overweight, high-school unlimited weight class wrestler, I had seen these vicious Lilliputians wrestle at close range. Gordon had been our summary judgment chief in a number of big cases and then, most recently, in a successful antitrust case where we had represented one of Rupert Murdoch's Internet companies against AOL.

Gordon began the brutal summary judgment project while he was still in San Francisco finishing off numerous high-level depositions of Visa and Andersen executives. He had to take some of the depositions originally assigned to me, because Visa/MasterCard were playing games to prevent me from deposing certain executives. By the end of the three-year discovery period, the defendants had finally realized that their executives were treating me like their father-confessor. With this tardy realization, the games began.

For example, in San Francisco, less than an hour prior to the scheduled deposition of Visa's "Debit Czar," Tony McEwen, I was informed that Mr. McEwen was apparently having a "heart attack." When I had to return to New York to finalize our expert reports, another lawyer was left to depose a quickly and miraculously recovered McEwen. The games continued during expert discovery, with defendants refusing to set a schedule where I could depose their economists, Ben Klein and George Benston, and also defend our economist, Frank Fisher. I chose to take the depositions of the defendants' experts, leaving Professor Fisher's defense to George Sampson.

Both sides moved for summary judgment. When a party asks for "partial" summary judgment, it is asking the court to take away certain claims or defenses from the other side before trial. A party seeking total summary judgment is asking the court to declare it the winner and cancel the trial. A party can ask for total summary judgment but also say that if the court won't do that, then at least please strip the other side of certain claims or defenses before the case goes to trial. Visa and MasterCard moved for both total and partial summary judgment. We asked Judge Gleeson to grant judgment for the merchants on the tying claim and most of the attempt-to-monopolize claim, leaving for the jury a little of that second claim and the big question of how much in damages should be awarded to the merchants. Though there was virtually no chance that our extreme and brazen request would be granted (and, according to popular opinion, little chance of our winning anything on summary judgment), I was concerned that Judge Gleeson might give us exactly what we asked for.

The three initial rounds of our summary judgment submissions are the finest written product I have worked on in 37 years of law practice. Our summary judgment evidence was so deep, so powerful and so skillfully marshaled by Gordon and our team, that I convinced myself that we could be left with only a damage case to put on at trial. This might hurt us because Judge Gleeson would then schedule a much shorter trial and not allow us to show the jury most of the evidence demonstrating Visa/MasterCard's venality. This included the evidence that was extensively quoted in newspapers after Judge Gleeson unsealed the record, evidence of the defendants' treachery and contempt for the welfare of consumers and merchants that might motivate the jury to award the merchants billions of dollars in damages. Without seeing and hearing this evidence, Visa/MasterCard's already-proven liability might seem technical and lack context for the jury. The jury might make a modest award of damages or, worse, award only nominal damages. Nominal damage awards of $1 or other very low figures have frequently been made in antitrust cases. A jury finds that the defendant has violated the antitrust laws but concludes that the plaintiff was not seriously damaged. This happened to the United States Football League when it "won" its antitrust case against the NFL. This can also happen when a jury, in effect, says, "A plague on both your houses." With Visa/MasterCard expected to scream "big/ bad Wal-Mart" early and often, I needed to put on a full trial of the evidence, showing how badly Visa/MasterCard had treated consumers and stores, both large and small.

With the briefing schedule for summary judgment in place, C&P went to the mattresses. Gordon moved into C&P's offices for the duration. He slept and showered at the firm most nights, and I, for several crucial weeks, not only moved out of the office but left the United States for Asia. Sarah, my older daughter, and Isaac, my son, had been studying in different regions of India during the first half of 2000. Isaac was a junior at Williams College, and Sarah was in a gap year, between high school and Williams.

Having two kids in India at that time made Jan and me nervous. India and Pakistan were, as usual, on the brink of war. Hindu/Muslim strife was occurring in many regions of the sub-continent. We had planned for almost a year to go there with our younger daughter, Elizabeth, meet Isaac and Sarah in Delhi, travel through India and Nepal and see that all five of us were returned to what we all complacently thought of as the safe United States. The unanticipated briefing schedule created one of those moments, pitting work versus family.

I opted for family that time, but with several emotional security blankets. I made Gordon give me a complete draft of our opening brief before I departed. I also made him promise that each and every change and comment, which I would send from India, would be reflected in the final work product. While in India and Nepal, I worked at night and sometimes through the night. I worked on trains and in the huts and teahouses of Nepal. In the Annapurna Valley I worked by flashlight, long after the generators were shut off in the middle of the evenings.

The result of all my edits, revisions and comments was over 700 handwritten pages . These changes, insertions, comments, harangues and exhortations were faxed in three parts from Delhi, Katmandu and Pokhara to Gordon at the price of $7.00 per page. Two years later, when I was in Bentonville, Arkansas, for one of the many meetings with Wal-Mart, I was introduced to several lawyers on what they call "The Wal-Mart Legal Team." When they heard my name, they said in chorus, "You're the guy who sent the $5,000 fax." And I said, "Wal-Mart ought to get on its hands and knees and kiss my feet for having the dedication to work that hard while in Asia, so I could send that $5,000 fax."

I returned from India on June 2, 2000, expecting that the opening summary judgment briefs had been finalized and that ours incorporated the essence of my 700-page annotated tantrum and would be filed later that day. Instead, once again, the defendants had requested, and been granted, another delay by Judge Gleeson. Before all the briefs were filed, the defendants asked for, and were given, two more extensions by Judge Gleeson. The final schedule called for the three rounds of briefing to occur on June 7, July 5 (Judge Gleeson's revenge), and July 31, with oral argument to occur four days later. By the time these summary judgment submissions were complete, they included more than 60,000 pages of briefs, declarations, affidavits, documents, deposition testimony and statements asserting and disputing that certain things were "undisputed."

But after this Herculean effort, including the renaming of C&P's changing room to the "Schnell Shower" to commemorate Gordon's heroic period of residency, the oral argument did not occur on August 4. The Second Circuit had granted the defendants the right to appeal Judge Gleeson's class-certification order. That made it impossible to begin the trial on November 27, 2000. Under the circuit's glacial procedures, the appeal wasn't even argued until February 5, 2001. Judge Gleeson postponed the trial and oral argument dates and said that new dates would not be set until after the class-certification issue had been resolved, including Visa/MasterCard's expected trip to the United States Supreme Court.

As the parties filed the third round of summary judgment submissions on July 31, 2000, we still didn't know whether we could rely on Andersen's Shark. I believed that The Shark standing (or swimming) alone would deliver a knockout punch and make it unlikely that the defendants would get anything out of their summary judgment motions. After that July 31, 2000 filing, the voluminous summary judgment submissions, which both sides had almost killed themselves to complete under Judge Gleeson's brutal schedule, were put into a time capsule.

But after two years of delay, we returned to court on June 21, 2002, right after the Supreme Court denied Visa/MasterCard's petition seeking review and the reversal of the class-certification order. On that same day, Judge Gleeson ordered most of the court file unsealed in response to the motion made by the *Wall Street Journal*. Judge Gleeson set a new trial date of April 28, 2003, and set a date in December 2002, later changed to January 10, 2003, for arguing the summary judgment motions.

At the defendants' request and over our objection, Judge Gleeson permitted an additional round of expert reports, an additional round of expert depositions and a fourth round of summary judgment briefs and supporting documentation. On December 13, 2002, two and one-half years after the parties completed their submission of more than 60,000 pages of summary judgment briefing and exhibits, the parties supplemented these with an additional 10,000 pages.

Oral argument was scheduled for January 10, 2003. The largest courtroom in the old federal courthouse, at Cadman Plaza in Brooklyn, had been selected as the arena. Our technicians had worked for a week to "wire" this old room with large video screens and all the gizmos necessary to project the multimedia presentation I was prepared to make. Judge Gleeson had allocated only 90 minutes for each side to distill what it took 70,000 pages to say in writing. In a case where I thought nothing would surprise me, the defendants' presentation on January 10, 2003, did.

I was not surprised that the defendants would divide their precious 90 minutes for oral argument, even though this was a bad idea. Two years before, they had divided the 30 minutes allotted by the Second Circuit, probably because one of the associations would have lost face if it had ceded to the other association the exclusive role of doing a high-profile argument. In planning for both the 2001 and 2003 arguments, Visa and MasterCard probably thought it was harder to pretend to be competitors if one lawyer did the oral argument for both.

It did surprise me a little that having divided in two their 90 minutes for arguing summary judgment, MasterCard went the extra step of inserting a third lawyer to argue part of its 45 minutes. The big surprise was that after more than six years of litigation and three years of planning for this day, the defendants, who are among the most media-savvy companies, arrived in court with a low-tech/no-tech presentation, virtually devoid of video, audio, or cyber-technology aides.

We went to court with a high-tech presentation that would allow me to illustrate every point I made with a Visa or MasterCard executive or expert testifying on two huge video screens. The defendants' executives would confirm that what I said was true, and show that what the defendants said was false. These talking heads were synchronized with defendants' documents and scrolling transcripts of their deposition testimony. The documents and transcripts were highlighted and popped up and out at the viewer in compelling and entertaining ways. For example, when the courtroom saw and heard a witness testifying at her deposition, there also would be a scrolling transcript of that testimony. If she referred to a document, an image would pop up on another screen, highlighting the part of the document she was talking about.

With the assistance of outside consultants and two technical wizards at C&P, Jon Shaman and Jason Lipton, we had a multimedia presentation ready to roll and ready to counter what we expected would be a polished high-tech presentation by the defendants. After all, Visa and MasterCard are companies that yearly sell hundreds of millions of additional revolving credit cards to Americans who already have them and are already deeply in debt. They do this by using slick commercials that say that MasterCard isn't really selling high-priced credit, but invaluable moments of family togetherness. Visa's ads say that its mission is to take shoppers anywhere they want to go, without mentioning that the final stop is frequently the bankruptcy court. To be fair, it must be said that Visa and MasterCard have actually eliminated that last stop for many consumers by successfully lobbying for legislation that will make it impossible to discharge most revolving credit card debt in bankruptcy proceedings.

The defendants argued first on January 10, 2003, in a courtroom that could not accommodate the scores of reporters, lawyers, friends and family who had come to witness the highly anticipated and long-delayed showdown. I will not spend much time on what they said, because three months later all of their 14 motions for summary judgment were denied in their entirety. By the time I got up to argue, I knew that the defendants had come to court with nothing but the arguments in their briefs. I would soon demonstrate that these arguments were falsehoods, using the defendants' own documents and testimony as my proof.

Our multimedia show had been refined in numerous practice sessions in front of our clients and C&P staff and in one trial simulation. Although our entire show was five hours long, I was able to use most of it in my 90 minutes by editing on the fly with Jason and Jon's help. We had compiled 71 distinct thematic groupings of documents, video clips and trial graphics to make specific points. These could be sifted and shortened, depending upon the needs of the moment. We had given these 71 groupings names like "Andersen Is Visa's Arms and Legs," "Klein [Visa's economist] Admits Visa is Forcing Merchants," "MasterCard and Visa Asked The Regionals to Abandon the Debit Market," "Visa Lies About Its Honor All Cards Rule," and "MasterCard Lies About Its No Steering Rule." "Looks Like a Credit Card" was a montage of bank commercials not only bragging that Visa debit cards looked like credit cards, but one in which the voice in the commercial jokes about how the merchant will think that the debit card is a credit card. Certain key documents and video clips were multi-image issue sequences unto themselves. Andersen's Shark had his own 13-image sequence. "Wes' Vote," where former Visa executive Wesley Tallman admits that he took a vote of Visa bankers in 1991 to "wait and be sued," had its own three-part presentation of video clips synchronized with a handwritten document recording the vote.

The transcript of the hearing reflects me asking for each thematic grouping by name. For example, I tell Jason, "Put the Shark Up," and later I say, "Let's show the Face of the Earth," one of our thematic groupings showing several PIN debit network executives testifying about the many tactics Visa was using to destroy their businesses.

The defendants spent a good portion of their 90 minutes repeating their argument that merchants got extra ("incremental") sales when they accepted debit cards. Visa and MasterCard argued that merchants were actually helped by the tying arrangements but that different merchants were helped to different degrees. They argued that this differential impact meant that the merchants had suffered no damages and they also argued that there should not be a class. At every step, the defendants tried to reargue the class ruling, which they had already lost three times.

Before I got to the lectern to begin my argument, I swatted away one of the closing arguments made by Steve Bomse for Visa. He had said that PIN debit couldn't be superior, as we claimed, because it couldn't be used in fancy restaurants. When Judge Gleeson asked why, Bomse responded that using a PIN pad would be "tacky" at a gracious dining establishment. So, as I strolled to the lectern, I sarcastically observed:

> **"You can use your online PIN debit card up in Canada, which means the restaurants up there are tacky or the entire country is tacky...."**
>
> **JUDGE GLEESON:** "The restaurants we go to are tacky."

I started my formal argument with a grouping of video and documents showing Visa and MasterCard experts and executives testifying that there was no evidence that debit cards increased sales. Professor Schmalensee was shown testifying that he hadn't "seen any such studies [showing incremental sales]" and that "for purposes of this analysis it didn't seem particularly important." On the screen,

Janet Crane, MasterCard's head of interchange, was shown testifying that she had not seen any proof of incremental sales. Another Visa economist, Orley Ashenfelter, assured the packed courtroom that he hadn't seen any proof of incremental sales but that he would have "if it existed or they [Visa] could find them." For good measure, I threw in the video of Steve Cole, the head of the Cash Station debit network in Chicago, testifying that "there was no evidence to support [incremental sales]. There continues to be no evidence that it results in incremental sales."

I showed this testimony of a regional debit network executive because the defendants had emphasized the fact that the regional debit networks were not suing Visa/MasterCard, despite our allegations that the defendants were trying to destroy them. To counter this argument, ATM/debit network executives were shown rebutting the defendants' arguments at every turn.

Judge Gleeson gave me a perfect opening when he asked, "Your adversary says the regionals aren't complaining. What accounts for that?" I instructed Jason to project on the large video screens "Face of The Earth," a grouping of testimony and documents from Regional ATM/debit network executives, which included Ron Congemi, the CEO of the STAR network, testifying that Visa had made it very clear that it wanted to eliminate STAR "from the face of the Earth." Next up was Stan Paur, the CEO of the PULSE debit network, testifying that he believed that the "Visa Check II program was an apparent effort to destroy regional EFT programs." EFTs are electronic funds transfers, meaning debit and ATM transactions. We showed an analysis from the MAC debit network stating that "off-line debit, an inferior and far more costly product, has quickly moved from a minority share of the national general purpose POS debit card market to dominance over online's safer, faster and far less costly service."

We played a video of MasterCard President Alan Heur testifying that he had met with executives of STAR, NYCE, PULSE and HONOR, the four largest regional debit networks, and offered each a deal in which they would abandon their debit network business in return for doing other work for MasterCard.

To demonstrate malice, intent and consumer harm, we showed a thematic grouping in which Visa set out to force the regional networks to raise their prices. These higher prices are paid by merchants and ultimately by consumers. Then, with interactive graphics, we explained how prices increased by over 2,000 percent in three distinct time periods following specific MasterCard and Visa conduct. We also showed Visa documents stating that forcing the regional networks to raise their prices was Visa's primary objective in offering the new Visa Check II debit card. One document said, "Even if product is never successful, you have earned your spurs. Regionals will increase cost."

One thematic grouping featured numerous Visa and Andersen executives testifying that Visa focused its missionary efforts at getting banks to stop issuing competing debit cards on "five or six key banks that represented the majority of the business." This testimony was repeated over and over again by witnesses who identified the Bank of America, Banc One, U.S. Bank, Norwest, First Union and Wachovia as the key banks. The same executives testified that these "five or six key banks" had been selected to set in motion a "domino effect" "project domino" and a "snowball effect" in which the smaller banks would emulate the larger banks and stop doing business with the competing regional debit networks.

The repetition of the same names and same words over and over again by every witness and in every document probably had the same effect on Judge Gleeson that it had on every group we showed it to. The evidence screamed *conspiracy*. It reminded me of the witnesses in the classic Costa Gavras movie *Z* all telling the inspector that when the assailant pounced on the victim he looked "lithe and fierce like a tiger."

Accounts of the famous trial following the tragic Triangle Shirtwaist Fire discuss how the jury was heavily influenced by the repetition of identical phrases by numerous witnesses. A similar effect was produced by a thematic grouping where several Visa and Andersen executives all testified that Andersen was acting as Visa's "arms and legs." It was important to show that Andersen was not only Visa's limbs, but also part of its brain so that Visa could not distance itself from The Shark's analysis shown in 13 images.

The last page of The Shark predicted that Visa By-law 2.10(e) would be "invalidated." The December 1997 date on The Shark, which I highlighted for Judge Gleeson, was ten months before the Department of Justice sued to invalidate that Visa by-law and a virtually identical MasterCard policy. This prediction, underlined in my argument, suggested that Visa was a lawless organization. This was a good argument to make to a judge who had spent most of his career in the Department of Justice. An equally valid interpretation of the Andersen prediction was that Judge Gleeson would declare the Visa by-law invalid in the Merchants' case. We had asserted that this Visa by-law and the similar MasterCard policy blocked Discover and American Express from entering the debit card market, while proclaiming that Visa and MasterCard were not competitors. Either interpretation—that Visa had been told in 1997 that it would lose the Merchants' case or that it had been told that it would lose another future case by the Department of Justice or lose both (as it eventually did)—would likely demean Visa in the eyes of Judge Gleeson, because it was enforcing a policy that it knew was illegal.

Ken Gallo, one of MasterCard's lawyers, had argued that our claim of conspiracy had no basis. So, I showed a MasterCard document stating that Visa and MasterCard had agreed to remove their debit card names "Electron" and "MasterCard II" from their debit cards, and played a video of MasterCard executive Edward Hogan testifying that "there was an agreement made with Visa...that we [MasterCard] would not use the Roman numeral II."

I then projected a document memorializing a Visa/MasterCard "Rules Alignment" meeting that showed that the first rules on the agenda for alignment were Visa and MasterCard's "Honor All Cards" tying arrangement rules. These rules were the focal point of the Merchants' case. We also projected two documents, one from Visa and one from MasterCard, both dated August 15, 1997. The Visa document showed Visa reducing the budget for promoting PIN debit to zero. The MasterCard document showed MasterCard removing all financial support for PIN debit in the United States. Both companies had eliminated funding for the faster, safer and cheaper product on the same day.

In a thematic grouping, designed to highlight Visa/MasterCard conspiracy, I explained what had happened when MasterCard had tried to adopt a debit strategy different from Visa's. We showed Visa's harsh criticism of MasterCard's strategy. We showed that this criticism was sent to banks on Visa's board of directors, reminding them that they were among the biggest issuers of MasterCard credit cards and explaining why MasterCard's reckless strategy would hurt the banks. We spotlighted the fact that this *Visa* analysis was marked "highly confidential" but had been produced to us from *MasterCard's* files. We demonstrated how, after this episode, MasterCard did a 180-degree "about face," falling into lockstep with Visa's debit strategy.

Some of these thematic groupings were used to demonstrate that the defendants actually agreed with our analysis of why and how their conduct damaged the merchants. The "Berlin" series featured documents from Visa meetings in Germany in the early 1990s, where

Andersen had predicted that unless the regional debit networks were "contained" and forced to abandon their low pricing to merchants, Visa/MasterCard and their banks would lose $813 million in credit card revenues annually.

We used some of these thematic groupings to show how successful the defendants had been in reducing the ability of stores to distinguish debit cards from credit cards. This evidence rebutted the defense that stores could identify signature debit cards and "steer" shoppers away from using them. One grouping included Visa and MasterCard executives Bruce McElhinney, Arman Khachadourian, Irene Katen, Linda Gage and Des Docherty testifying that they didn't know of any way for a merchant to visually distinguish their debit cards from their credit cards.

In another attack on the defendants' steering defense, I projected the first page of an article about rising *credit card rates* in the *Wall Street Journal*, which included a picture of a MasterCard signature *debit card*. I pointed out that the *Wall Street Journal* was following the case very closely and had published three front-page articles about the case in the previous year. The *Journal* had made the motion that unsealed the court file. However, even the *Journal* couldn't tell the difference between MasterCard's credit cards and debit cards. This line of argument caused laughter in the courtroom.

Three months later, when Judge Gleeson granted most of our summary judgment request, he denied our request to strike the steering defense. Was all that effort directed at the defendants' steering defense a waste of time? I don't believe so. The points were scored, and Visa/MasterCard's credibility was diminished in Judge Gleeson's and the public's eyes. The steering defense was in tatters as we went to trial. The defensive line coaches at Williams College told us to knock down every opposing player who crossed our paths, and never to run around blocks trying to get to the ball carrier. They taught us that if everyone just hit anyone with the opposing color jersey, the ball carrier would get knocked down. "If you do everything, you will win."

At one point in the argument, I told Judge Gleeson that certain defense arguments were "fabricated" and an "affront to the court." To back up this statement, we played the video of MasterCard former CEO Pete Hart, testifying that MasterCard had a no steering rule when Hart was CEO, but after a break, the video showed Hart recanting and saying that he changed his testimony because Noah Hanft, MasterCard's U.S. Counsel, had told Hart that he was "confused." This was the same video that had gotten Magistrate Judge Mann so annoyed during the December 1999 settlement conference.

As a bookend to the Hart testimony, we showed testimony from Robert Miller, the former head of Visa's rules department. At his deposition, Miller was asked why a clear "change" in Visa's anti-steering rules was being called a "clarification" by Visa. Uncomfortably, the head of rules said over and over again that Paul Allen, Visa's General Counsel, was the only person at Visa who could explain why the obvious alteration in the Visa rules was being "positioned" as merely a "clarification." After this deposition, Visa changed Miller's job title.

To give further definition to the negative image I was sketching of the defendants, I showed Judge Gleeson a 1987 document where MasterCard vitriolically criticized the same steering argument that MasterCard and Visa had just spent most of their 90 minutes pitching to him. In the 1987 document, MasterCard had berated the proponent of this steering argument, Booz Allen Hamilton, a consultant that had been retained by Visa and MasterCard. In the document, MasterCard lashed out at Booz Allen, saying:

"We don't accept that and we don't believe an arbitrator or a jurist would either. In fact, while you make that statement to us in person, it is highly unlikely that such a claim would be made by MasterCard in its own defense in a court."

After letting that sink in, I looked Judge Gleeson right in the eyes and said, "I don't know how to put this, Your Honor, but they think you are that credulous jurist who would accept this inane argument, which they rejected as being a fallacious argument 15 years ago." Gleeson, who is skilled at controlling his emotions and facial gestures, looked back at me with a colorless stare.

The last images shown to Judge Gleeson were meant to leave him with a simpler, but more sinister, picture of the defendants, the one I had formed. Visa and MasterCard were companies that clearly saw what was good and bad for common people, and chose to do them harm, when that served the interests of the bank cartel. I believed that this picture of the defendants would offend John Gleeson more than merely proving that Visa and MasterCard thought that he would accept a specious defense or that they had intentionally violated the antitrust laws. It offended me more.

To show the defendants' contempt for common people, we showed another analysis prepared by Andersen for Visa. It broke down the debit card market into various pricing options, strategies and trends. It rated each of these as "positive," "neutral" or "negative" for the various stakeholders, including MasterCard, Visa, the regional debit networks, consumers and stores. Over and over again, the analysis said that what was bad for consumers, stores and competition was good for Visa and MasterCard and vice versa.

The summary judgment hearing was widely covered in the legal and trade press during the following weeks, including a review of the cyber techniques that we had used in the courtroom. Months later, the London-based *Economist* magazine reported on the settlement saying, "At a rather theatrical hearing in January, Mr. Constantine persuaded the presiding judge, John Gleeson, that Wal-Mart's case was mostly already won." As the argument ended on January 10, 2003, that also was my feeling. Judge Gleeson ended the hearing by praising all the lawyers. He said that the "briefs are excellent, the oral arguments even better all around...the lawyering is fantastic." Those words were the most generous I had heard from the bench during more than 30 years of practice.

That was Judge Gleeson's public statement, reported the next week in the *New York Law Journal*. However, what he said to us privately a few minutes later was much more important. Judge Gleeson's law clerk, Carter Burwell, quietly came over to the lawyers at the end of the hearing and told us the judge wanted to speak with us in chambers. Once we reassembled, Judge Gleeson praised us again, this time even more effusively. He told us how much he was looking forward to a trial with such great lawyers, in such a great and historic case. Gleeson then delivered a threat. He said, "Nevertheless, I strongly, strongly recommend that you settle this case not just before trial, but before I issue my summary judgment decision."

Both sides understood that this was a threat. I, full of myself and in the afterglow of what virtually everyone who had witnessed the argument viewed as a public humiliation of Visa/MasterCard, was sure that Judge Gleeson was threatening the defendants. However, the Visa and MasterCard lawyers believed that Judge Gleeson was threatening us. In the following week, both sides told Eric Green that Gleeson had threatened the other side. Green was the mediator whom the parties had jointly hired to facilitate some necessary, though likely futile, settlement discussions. The Green mediation sessions had begun in the late fall of 2002.

On April 1, 2003, the evening after Judge Gleeson issued his summary judgment decision, Eric Green reached me on my cell phone at a homeless shelter, where I was spending the night accompanied by my former McDermott Will & Emery partner Larry Fox. All Green said to me was, "I guess you were right about who Gleeson was threatening. I'll talk to you tomorrow." As the *American Banker* of April 7, 2003, reported, "[a] summary judgment decision handed down Wednesday may have seemed like a bad April Fool's Day joke to Visa and MasterCard, which lost all their motions while the retailers won most of theirs." Judge Gleeson's succinct 16-page decision resolved 22 pending motions, 19 seeking summary judgment and three others attempting to shape the contours of the trial to begin 27 days later, on April 28, 2003.

When a party moves for summary judgment, it is asking the judge to rule that an issue, which the jury would normally decide, has already been decided—arguing that "no rational juror could decide otherwise." In his decision, Judge Gleeson denied Visa/MasterCard's summary judgment motion, asserting that they had proven (and therefore that no rational juror could disagree) that credit cards and debit cards were the same thing, or, stated in antitrust parlance, that credit cards and debit cards were a "single product." *o for 1*

Judge Gleeson denied defendants' motion seeking judgment that they were not tying debit cards to credit cards, legally or illegally. *o for 2*

Judge Gleeson denied defendants' motion seeking judgment that credit cards were part of a market that included all other forms of payment. *o for 3*

Judge Gleeson denied defendants' motion seeking judgment that Visa/MasterCard lacked the market power necessary to force stores to accept their debit card transactions. *o for 4*

Judge Gleeson denied defendants' motion seeking judgment that

Visa and MasterCard could not have conspired to enforce their tying arrangements. *0 for 5*

Judge Gleeson denied defendants' motion for judgment that the merchants had no standing to sue them for attempting and conspiring to monopolize the debit card market. *0 for 6*

Judge Gleeson denied MasterCard's motion for judgment that it could not be charged with attempting to monopolize the debit card market, because MasterCard was too puny. *0 for 7*

Judge Gleeson denied defendants' motion for judgment that they had not engaged in predatory or anticompetitive conduct. *0 for 8*

Judge Gleeson denied defendants' motion for judgment that Visa/MasterCard did not have "specific intent" to monopolize the debit card market. *0 for 9*

Judge Gleeson denied defendants' motion for judgment that Visa/MasterCard were not "dangerously close" to monopolizing the debit card market. *0 for 10*

Judge Gleeson denied defendants' motion for judgment that Visa/MasterCard had not conspired to monopolize the debit card market. *0 for 11*

Judge Gleeson denied defendants' motion for judgment that the merchants' claim for money damages and the theory and methodology that the merchants offered to prove their damages was irrational. *0 for 12*

In addition to completely denying these 12 Visa/MasterCard motions for summary judgment, Judge Gleeson also denied MasterCard's motion for a "severance," seeking a separate trial from Visa. He also denied the defendants' motion requesting a so-called *James Hearing*, where they would seek to exclude certain evidence against a particular defendant that they said would prejudice the jury against the other defendant. *0 for 13 and 14*

Judge Gleeson granted the merchants' summary judgment motion on the first and most crucial element of the tying claim. He held that no rational jury could fail to find that credit cards and debit cards were two distinct products. *1 for 1*

Judge Gleeson granted our motion for judgment that the sale of these two distinct products had been tied together by Visa and MasterCard. *2 for 2*

Judge Gleeson granted our motion for judgment that the tying arrangements affected a substantial amount of interstate business activity. *3 for 3*

Judge Gleeson granted our motion for judgment that the sale of credit and charge card services to merchants was a relevant market. *4 for 4*

Judge Gleeson granted our motion for judgment that Visa had market power in the credit and charge card market. *5 for 5*

Judge Gleeson denied our motion for the same judgment with respect to MasterCard, leaving that determination initially for the jury. *5 for 6*

Judge Gleeson granted our motion for judgment that there is a market for the sale of debit card services to merchants. *6 for 7*

In addition to determining our summary judgment motions, Judge Gleeson also denied our motion to strike the defendants' steering defense, leaving to the jury the issue of whether stores could identify defendants' debit cards and steer shoppers away from using them, thereby reducing the amount of damage they suffered as a result of the defendants' tying arrangements. *6 for 8*

The magnitude of this result is not adequately conveyed by this o for 14 versus 6 for 8 scorecard. It is difficult to get summary judgment in any complex case, because courts are extremely reluctant to make a decision that juries are normally supposed to make. It becomes much harder to get summary judgment when the discovery record is large, because no matter how much proof is marshaled by the side seeking summary judgment, the party opposing summary judgment can usually point to some evidence in the record contradicting it. And just a little contrary evidence will defeat the motion. When there is conflicting evidence, it is hard for the judge to say that "no rational juror" could disagree with the court's finding on that issue. Our case had produced not just a big discovery record, the pretrial documentation and deposition testimony was mammoth. The 400 deposition transcripts alone revealed some conflicting evidence on virtually every imaginable issue in the case.

Summary judgment has become a tool used almost exclusively by defendants in antitrust cases, not by plaintiffs. This is now so ingrained in the law that Judge Gleeson began his decision with the observation and citation that "...*plaintiffs* are not required to overcome any 'special burden' when '*opposing* summary judgment in an antitrust case' and 'can defeat the motion by coming forward with specific facts to show a genuine issue exists requiring a trial.'" Judge Gleeson's clerk probably couldn't find a quote framing the legal issue in the other way, that is, how little evidence is necessary for a *defendant* to defeat a plaintiff's motion for summary judgment. Why? Because plaintiffs rarely try to get summary judgment in antitrust cases, and when they try, the effort is not taken seriously. When the defendants perceived that the threat Judge Gleeson made after oral argument on January 10, 2003, was directed at the plaintiffs, they were reasoning conventionally. Visa/MasterCard hadn't paid enough attention to the mountain range of evidence we had accumulated during the discovery process.

Finally, and more important than the scorecard or our beating the odds, was the extraordinary content of the ruling. On top of all the key issues that we went into trial having already won, the judge had sowed a minefield for Visa/MasterCard. On the other hand, he had laid out a gentle golf course with a series of "tap-ins" awaiting us at each green.

In granting our credit card market power motion against Visa, but leaving this decision to the jury with respect to MasterCard, Judge Gleeson had set up such a tap-in. By 2003, MasterCard had virtually pulled even with Visa in credit card statistics. MasterCard selectively publicized certain numbers that made MasterCard look even bigger than it was. We would show the jury MasterCard documents, where they proclaimed that they had replaced Visa as the number-one credit card network. Convincing the jury that MasterCard had market power, when they had already been instructed by Judge Gleeson that Visa had market power, was a tap-in. If MasterCard were to resist this too much, after publicly claiming that they were number one, they would risk further eroding their credibility with the jury.

Judge Gleeson constructed another minefield/tap-in situation in denying Visa/MasterCard's summary judgment motion concerning the issue of defendants' "dangerous probability" of getting monopoly power in the debit card market. Gleeson observed that Visa's debit card market share, by itself, was enough to defeat their motion and that if the jury found that Visa and MasterCard had acted in concert, he would direct a verdict against the defendants on this issue.

On the issue of acting conspiratorially, Judge Gleeson fired numerous warning shots. He perfunctorily and impatiently denied the defendants' motion to dismiss the conspiracy-to-monopolize claim with two words: "I disagree." Similarly, in denying Master-Card's motion to dismiss our claim that MasterCard along with Visa was attempting to monopolize the debit card market, Judge Gleeson cited "common ownership, a lack of competition, and incidents of concerted activity by the two defendants...." And in rejecting the defendants' motion to throw out our attempt- and conspiracy-to-monopolize claims for lack of standing, Judge Gleeson pointed to the "direct and circumstantial evidence" from which a jury could find conspiracy.

Judge Gleeson also pointed out that he wasn't about to waste his time reconsidering Visa/MasterCard arguments about the economic implausibility of our damage case. Gleeson had already rejected these arguments at the class motion stage. The defendants had tried to get another shot at winning this fight. Though they technically had the right to try, the reality was that once these arguments were rejected in the class certification decision, the subsequent defeats were virtually automatic. Failing to understand this, Visa/MasterCard later tried and failed a third and fourth time.

Finally, in virtually giving us victory on the tying arrangement claims before trial, but withholding a complete victory, Judge Gleeson actually gave us everything we needed, while denying us something that we half-wanted but knew would actually hurt us. Had Judge Gleeson given us complete summary judgment on the tying claims, the trial would have been shortened, and we likely would have been precluded from showing the jury much of the evidence on liability. This evidence was likely to convince the jury that the defendants were not only lawbreakers but venal and responsible for extensive harm to stores and consumers. This was the evidence that would motivate the jury to punish Visa/MasterCard with a massive monetary verdict.

Writing about the decision in the *American Banker* of April 4, 2003, the former General Counsel of Citibank's card business, Duncan MacDonald, said, "It's hard to imagine that the associations can now win." However, it was my job to imagine that the defendants could still win, and to prevent it from happening. Adversaries are often most dangerous when they are badly wounded. So, we got ready for the defendants' final pretrial assaults, and they soon came.

Visa/MasterCard's Hail Marys

———

O N APRIL 14, 2003, two weeks after the summary judgment decision and two weeks prior to trial, Visa/MasterCard filed 31 motions. Twenty-eight were *"motions in-limine"* asking Judge Gleeson to prevent us from using most of the evidence we wanted to present at trial. They also filed three more *Daubert* motions seeking to exclude most of our expert testimony.

Those who have read this far know that both the *motions in-limine* and the *Daubert* motions were a second and, in some instances, a third attempt to prevent us from putting our case before a jury. Most of these motions were particularly silly because they were seeking to exclude the same evidence that Judge Gleeson had relied upon only two weeks earlier in denying all of Visa/MasterCard's summary judgment requests and granting most of ours. By virtue of their sheer number, these motions also smelled of desperation. On the same day, April 14, 2003, we filed six motions of our own. This number shrank to five when the defendants conceded the relief requested in one of ours.

Among the most desperate defense motions, and the most revealing to us because they spotlighted precisely what the defendants feared most (and had probably suffered from most, at their recent mock trials), were these: The defendants made a motion to exclude all evidence about consumer confusion over whether a Visa/Master-Card card was debit or credit. The defendants didn't want a jury (all undoubtedly consumers themselves) to see the MasterCard document showing that 72 to 78 percent of cardholders confused MasterCard credit with debit—and that MasterCard had known this and done nothing to alleviate this confusion, which caused bounced checks and other consumer harm. The Visa bookend was a document showing that the number-one reason cardholders first used a Visa debit card was their belief that it was a credit card. The defendants also made a motion to prevent us from showing the jury how Dean Richard Schmalensee, the economist used by both Visa and MasterCard on the class motion, had contradicted most of their defense.

Visa made two motions seeking to prevent us from using the "Berlin Series" and The Shark. Visa comically referred to these two analyses done by Andersen in 1990 and 1997 as the "*1990 Accenture Document*" and the "*1997 Accenture Document*." In 2002, Andersen had been convicted of criminal conduct and surrendered its accounting licenses for its key role in auditing abuses that led to the collapse of Enron. Some 85,000 jobs were lost in this debacle. Visa, probably with the benefit of mock trial results, knew how dangerous it was to allow a jury to hear the hated Andersen name so closely linked with Visa, and to hear Visa witnesses testify that Andersen was Visa's "arms and legs" in the debit business. Visa's solution was to use the "Accenture" name, which Andersen Consulting adopted years after it did these analyses for Visa and years after Andersen Consulting had separated from "Arthur Andersen," a name that also appeared on some of these documents. In an Orwellian fashion, Visa was trying not only to rename these documents, but to make believe that they never existed.

Ironically, Accenture was well on its way to becoming an equally hated name. Accenture's reincorporation in Bermuda and its much-publicized role as the consultant to many American firms outsourcing U.S. workers' jobs to third-world countries would likely have played badly with most juries.

On April 14, 2003, defendants also made a motion to prevent us from showing the jury two analyses done by Visa and MasterCard during the same week in July 1998, discussing how they could use their rules to destroy the competing STAR and HONOR ATM/debit networks. Various publications had already reported on and quoted from these documents after Judge Gleeson unsealed the court file in November 2002. As we expected, Visa also moved to prevent us from showing the jury documents or testimony relating to "Wes' Vote," the vote by a group of banks to "wait and be sued" taken at a 1991 meeting of the Visa debit advisors. The lawsuit that these bank advisors voted to wait and be sued in was the Merchants' case. For some reason, Visa didn't want the jurors in the Merchants' case to see those documents or testimony.

The schedule provided us with one week to respond to these 31 defense motions. We asked Judge Gleeson for three additional days. When he denied this modest request, I was pleased. As painful as it was for the people on our team assigned to oppose these motions, this was another clear signal from Judge Gleeson that as far as he was concerned, we were going to win. If he had had any intention of seriously considering any of the defense motions to limit our prerogatives at trial, he would have given us more time to respond. Judge Gleeson had recently delivered a similar signal by denying our request that the defendants be required to pare down the ridiculous list of trial exhibits they had submitted.

The defendants' trial exhibit list included more than 7,600 exhibits amounting to more than 180,000 pages. Judge Gleeson's refusal to make Visa/MasterCard reduce this list of potential evidence, which included 60,000 pages of trial exhibits that they hadn't provided to us during the discovery period, was his way of saying to us, "Don't worry." However, the judge's rejection of our earlier request and his denial of our request for 10 instead of seven days to respond to the 31 motions made on April 14, were his version of tough love. Someone had to deal with these grotesquely large and desperate defendant gambits, and it wasn't going to be me. By that time, I was working around the clock on trial preparation and settlement talks.

To respond to Visa/MasterCard's final pretrial assault, C&P assembled a team of 17 lawyers and a few paralegals from our firm and those assisting us. This team not only responded within the one-week deadline but actually made early responses to many of the defendants' motions. Matt Cantor, C&P's youngest partner, wrote 14 opposition briefs in this one week and did not lose a single motion.

Judge Gleeson decided the most important of these motions on April 28, the day trial was scheduled to begin and we actually picked a jury. That day, Gleeson decided eight of the defendants' motions, denying seven and granting one minor motion. On the same day, Judge Gleeson granted two of our five motions, the only two he decided. As Judge Gleeson read his decisions from the bench at 9:45 AM on April 28, 2003, we knew that our case was completely intact. We had won all six battles. The last two victories—Judge Gleeson's earlier summary judgment decision and these *in-limine* and *Daubert* decisions—left us a trial with the liability phase virtually over. All we really had to do was use the pretext of the small remaining parts of the liability trial to shower the jury with evidence of Visa/MasterCard's contempt for merchants, consumers and the law. This, by and large, was the same evidence that had turned the tide with Magistrate Judge Mann at her conference in December 1999 and had sealed the defendants' fate at summary judgment a few weeks before. Then, with this evidence fresh in the jurors' minds, we would put on our damage case through Professor Fisher, our economic expert, and ask the jury to award the merchants billions in damages. But there was one problem—a good one, but nevertheless a problem: Something had happened at 4:45 AM that morning, which caused the judge to send the seated jury home and tell us to return three days later on the morning of May 1, 2003, to make our opening arguments. My opening statement, the product of three years of personal trial preparation, would have to be redone. The carefully planned trial script would also have to be redone. Numerous changes had to be made in the case that we could and would put before the jury. We had a little over two days to reformulate a case that had taken almost seven years to put together.

I slept for five out of the next 60 hours and prepared a new opening. Our trial team reworked the entire trial script in those 60 hours. At C&P, it was the age of miracles.

PART III

—

Endgame

Preparing for Trial

F OR A PERIOD of time in the year 2000, we prepared for a trial scheduled to begin on November 27, 2000. We began to assemble witness lists, documents and portions of the videotaped depositions we would show to the jury. We actually began to prepare certain trial witnesses. We even conducted one trial simulation and scheduled a full mock trial for October 2000. However, when the Second Circuit mechanically acceded to Judge Gleeson's request that it review his class-certification decision and sloppily allowed the appeals procedures to drag on for 21 months, the possibility of a trial in the year 2000, or any time soon after, disappeared. Judge Gleeson told us he would not reschedule the trial until Visa/MasterCard had exhausted the appellate process, including the defendants' promised trip to the Supreme Court. That meant we would not have a trial until at least 2002 and, as it turned out, well into 2003.

This delay could have crushed us. But similar to our approach to the magistrate judge's refusal of our request to limit the scope of discovery and our response to the court's reopening of summary judgment, expert reports and expert depositions years after they concluded, we turned this additional problem into an advantage. We used the time to painstakingly put together a trial plan. We refined this plan and the trial script in numerous prep sessions and simulations performed for our clients, for eight additional mock juries and for the trial team audience at C&P, on many Saturday nights.

After the November 27, 2000, trial date was adjourned indefinitely, my personal trial preparation resumed on September 4, 2001. I know, as I write this date, that it conjures in my mind, and likely in the readers', the words and image "just one week before." Of course, I didn't know the world would change a week later or that preparing for trial would help me get through what happened on September 11, 2001.

On 9/11, I was on my way into C&P's Manhattan office, on Madison and 51st, diagonally across from the back of Saint Patrick's Cathedral, when I first heard the reports. At that point, only one tower had been hit. As the morning went on, C&P experienced the events as millions of other families did. Each few minutes brought another indelible image. I was on the phone with Eliot Spitzer five minutes after he witnessed the second plane hit the South Tower, as he was looking through his window in the Attorney General's office at 120 Broadway, a few hundred yards away from Ground Zero. Eliot and I had worked together in the South Tower back in 1982.

As a group, C&P watched the Twin Towers collapse and the streets of Nablus and East Jerusalem erupt in wild jubilation. Eliot called again to find out what was going on uptown, and I told him to gather his staff and "get the hell out of there." Eliot then led a contingent from the AG's office, who walked from Lower Manhattan to the Governor's New York City headquarters at 633 Third Avenue near 40th Street, where I would serve as his Senior Advisor years later.

Everybody at C&P was able to quickly and mercifully get in touch with their immediate families, except one lawyer, Stacey Mahoney. Carl, her husband, who worked near Ground Zero at Pine Street and Maiden Lane, appeared to be lost. Later he was found dazed, alive and physically unhurt. Still later, we were told that Neil Levin, a friend whom I had vacationed with weeks before, had perished after making sure that most of his staff at the Port Authority were safely evacuated from the North Tower. Right after that, we got word that Stacey Sanders, the daughter of John Sanders, one of C&P's clients, had perished while working for Marsh & McLennan in the North Tower. Within months, Alison Ross, a dazed young angel, would come to work with us at C&P on the Merchants' case. Her beloved father, Richard, had been on one of the planes flown into the towers. Alison's sister Abigail, Richard Ross's older daughter, also lost her best friend, Stacey Sanders, that day. The "more fortunate" New York families experienced and continued to experience September 11, 2001, in the horrendous but slightly removed manner that C&P did.

By 4:00 PM on 9/11, I turned back to the trial preparation project I had begun the week before and forced myself to go through the motions of working for awhile. The impulse that motivated me to do some work, or at least make believe, was the same as described by many friends and acquaintances. Our work, customs and rituals would see us through, and we wouldn't let "them" take that away. After that, I walked home with a close friend from Kaye Scholer who was afraid to walk home alone.

The next day, I had trouble concentrating on work. But with each succeeding day, it got easier. The nights were filled with CNN and NPR, but the days were my escape. Each person lucky enough to be spared the death or maiming of a loved one still needed an escape. This was mine, and while I was doing it, the escape was complete. Business ground to a standstill. The phone rang very little while I read, reread and analyzed the discovery record in the Merchants' case. I wrote and compiled three documents, which we called *The Log, Lloyd's Book* and *The Dialogue*.

The Log was a compilation of what I considered to be the most important documents in the case. First, I culled documents from the exhibits to the 39 depositions I had taken or defended. Since these depositions involved many of the most important witnesses, this was a good start. Later, I invited all C&P attorneys and paralegals working on the case to bring me what they considered the most important documents, good and bad. I eventually put more than 1,200 documents into The Log. I reread each document several times, highlighted the key portions and wrote a short narrative explanation of why each document was important. I formulated and named 57 issue codes, such as "defendants' market power" and "credit is a market." Each document was assigned one or more of these codes. The Log kept growing, and each C&P attorney and paralegal periodically received updated and refined electronic and hard copy versions of the document.

The Dialogue was made up of important extracts from the 400 depositions, with descriptions of each deposition extract in the form of a dialogue and debate between me and the other attorneys and paralegals at C&P. The Dialogue, which eventually amounted to several thousand pages, began when I asked C&P attorneys to nominate the ten best and ten worst deposition extracts involving the key themes and issues in the case. Through several rounds of "nominations," arguments and renominations, we compiled the 1,066 best and worst pieces of deposition testimony. I wrote a commentary on each, stating why I agreed or disagreed with a nomination. The lawyers replied to my commentary with their own comments. This led to additional nominations, commentaries and responses. The last version of The Dialogue had more than 1,300 deposition extracts with dueling commentary.

The third document, Lloyd's Book, was my narrative version of the Merchants' case organized around the elements of the merchants' two main claims against Visa/MasterCard, for illegal tying of debit to credit and attempted monopolization of the debit card market. In the last of many iterations, Lloyd's Book was a 650-page story script. The story contained the very best documents, deposition extracts and other evidence in the order we would attempt to present them at trial. I kept this work to myself and one other C&P attorney, Michelle Peters, for more than a year. Michelle moved into my office to help me write it. While sitting in front of our adjacent computers, I told Michelle that we were like Ferrante and Teicher, but she was too young to understand my reference to the wildly popular twin piano team that banged out famous movie themes and other standards on TV shows like Ed Sullivan's or Perry Como's. Every lawyer and paralegal at C&P had the later versions of Lloyd's Book. Several months were spent analyzing the authenticity and admissibility of each piece of evidence referenced in it.

More important than my personal trial preparation and self-therapy, was the preparation of the C&P trial team, who were joined by several lawyers whom we had selected from among the law firms assisting us. The trial team reconfigured the massive discovery record into a workable format. They reviewed roughly 500 deposition transcripts from our case and the United States' case against Visa/MasterCard, as well as the trial transcript from the U.S. case. They reviewed, again, the roughly one million pages of documents deemed "interesting" from more than five million pages originally produced.

Under the supervision of Bob Begleiter, the team wrote trial memos on each class representative, each defendant and each important third party. Trial memos were also written on topics such as "electronic commerce," "hardware vendors," and industry consultants such as Andersen Consulting and MasterCard's analogous alter ego, Edgar Dunn Associates. Each trial memo identified the witnesses, documents and deposition extracts that would tell this particular part of our story. Attorneys analyzed the authenticity and admissibility of the evidence and constructed a plan for introducing each piece of evidence at trial.

"Movie Night" became a regular event at C&P after the Supreme Court denied Visa/MasterCard's petition for certiorari in June 2002. Each attorney who took an important deposition made a movie from segments of the videotaped deposition, which we might show to the jury at trial. The first cuts were as long as three-hour epics and as brief as five-minute short subjects. The attorneys, often with the help of C&P's technical gurus, Jon Shaman, Jason Lipton and Kevin Potere, made these movies on their computer screens with movie clip creation software that C&P had purchased and modified ourselves during the case. Every lawyer and paralegal at C&P had hundreds of thousands of documents and hundreds of deposition transcripts and videos accessible on their computers. These could be sorted, sifted and searched by name, word, subject, or the 57 issue codes we created. The video images could be synchronized with documents and scrolling transcripts.

Each Movie Night, the attorney/director played his or her film for the trial team. We ripped the movie apart and conducted a group edit as we watched. In this process, watching and group-editing a five-minute movie could last thirty minutes, and a three-hour epic could take until midnight or beyond.

Movie nights, which began in June 2002, were eventually held four nights a week at our midtown office. After the group edit, the team watched the edited movie, and re-edited it as many times as was necessary to make it concise, comprehensible and compelling for a jury. We also knew that the defendants would "counter-designate" other portions of the same video depositions that they wanted to show the jury. Knowing this, we tried to include, in our movies, the parts of the depositions we thought the defendants would want to show. This would minimize disputes.

A year before trial, our attorneys resumed the drafting of trial testimony that had begun in 2000. We drafted testimony for 270 witnesses whom we might call to testify at trial. In reality, only a small percentage of our 270 and the defendants' 460 designated witnesses would have actually testified at the three-month trial.

We met with our key witnesses many times. They were scattered all around the country. I traveled to Phoenix three times to meet with one witness, Ralph Spurgin. Other trial witness preparation trips took me to Bentonville, Arkansas; Pleasanton, California; Richmond, Virginia; Hoffman Estates, Illinois; and Columbus, Ohio. I travelled to Washington, D.C. and Boston so many times that I left clothing and squash racquets in "lockers" I established in those cities. There also were shorter trips to local merchants who would testify for us. One of these was a manager at Fairway, the famous Upper West Side food market, where weekend shopping resembles the roller derby. Another trial witness I prepped several times was Barry Rosenberg, the owner of a tiny and beloved Lincoln Center area bakery named "Soutine."

The preparation of our expert witnesses was primarily done by my partner, Jeff Shinder, who is an economics wiz. This preparation began in 1997 and entailed many trips for Jeff to Toronto and Milwaukee and for both of us to Cambridge, Massachusetts. Trips to the Bay Area were my personal favorites. No matter how late I arrived, and how hectic the schedule was, I always got a thrill when the taxi passed Candlestick Park and approached downtown San Francisco. My ritual was to check into the old Clift Hotel, Room 1703, and take a shower in the uniquely strong water pressure that I discovered that room offered. I would put on a suit jacket, go down to the Redwood Room and have a drink while gazing at the massive Gustav Klimt reproductions on the walls, especially "The Kiss." Most of the time, this was a single drink, imbibed in solitude. But at times, I was joined by a colleague, a client, a stranger, and twice by Larry Popofsky, Visa's lead counsel.

My least favorite trips, but only at the end, were to Bentonville, Arkansas, the home of Wal-Mart. It's a tough place to get to. The trip was made easier during the course of the case by the construction of what is euphemistically called "Northwest Arkansas Regional Airport," two miles away from the "Wal-Mart Home Office." When these trips began, they were much harder to make but exciting and enjoyable. During one of those early trips to Bentonville, before the Wal-Mart airport was built, we traveled to Fayetteville through Memphis in an ice-storm. We got to hear someone from the maintenance crew shout, "Does anyone around here know how to de-ice the wings?" Later that night, Mitch Shapiro and I checked into a budget motel recommended by Wal-Mart, which prominently advertised the availability of massages, but warned that you couldn't get a "sexual massage." As the years dragged on, the trips became easier, and the accommodations and food better, but the relationship with Wal-Mart became tense.

In the year 2000, we conducted one trial simulation but canceled a full mock trial that had been scheduled for October 2000. After the resumption of trial preparation, we held a multiple-day trial simulation in February 2003 and a six-day mock trial in March 2003. It's hard to overstate the importance of these trial simulations and of doing them properly. It's easy to make yourself feel good by clobbering the other side in an unfair contest. It's hard to spend the time and money necessary to give the other side representation equal to or better than yours. When you do this, you get a real understanding of what a jury thinks about the case, and what each side must and therefore is expected to do in order to improve their chances of success.

I considered assigning myself to defend Visa. This was rejected because the rest of the team bluntly told me I was too closely identified with the merchants' point of view. They did not trust me to do the best job for the defendants. I disagreed but accepted their judgment.

After I was rejected, we assigned top-flight counsel to the defendants. I chose my partner, Bob Begleiter, the other elder statesman at C&P. Bob is, by far, our best and most experienced trial lawyer and the master litigator in our firm. At one simulation, we also assigned George Sampson to represent one of the defendants. While working for me in the Attorney General's office, George had won a large jury verdict in a bid-rigging case. Ronnie Mann, our magistrate judge, had been on the losing side. Female jurors liked the tall and good-looking George. We also retained Richard Emery and Andy Celli, two accomplished trial counsel, to represent the defendants. Richard is a famous civil liberties lawyer. In a landmark case, Richard had challenged and overturned the old New York City charter of government in the United States Supreme Court. Richard played the role of opposing counsel at two mock trials for our 1998 antitrust case against AOL. We knew that Richard was very effective at making odious and reprehensible business behavior seem common and acceptable.

In addition to providing the defendants with good counsel, we gave them all the other ingredients needed to mount a strong defense. They created expensive trial graphics and had state-of-the-art technology to formulate their presentations. Using these tools, they put together a case that bent and stretched the truth. This was what we expected from Visa/MasterCard at trial, because this is what they had done at the class and summary judgment contests. The defendants' case proved strong enough for one of the eight mock juries to deadlock, but at a point where a majority of the jurors were on the defendants' side and were physically threatening the minority of jurors holding out for the merchants.

We treated these simulations as if they were the real thing, especially the six-day mock trial. This was conducted outside New York City, in the town of Lynbrook in Nassau County. We moved to Long

Island for a week. We worked through most of the nights in the sleaziest motel I have stayed in since college. The blankets were so cheap that they created a static electricity light show when unfolded. Our clients and witnesses stayed at the fancy Garden City Hotel, nearby.

The length and complexity of the mock trial, and the use of live and real witnesses, movies, real experts for both sides, fancy interactive trial graphics and a former federal judge presiding in a wired courtroom, helped the mock jurors to willingly suspend disbelief. By the end of the week, most of the 40 jurors seemed to forget that it was a mock trial. This was demonstrated in many ways, including the spectacle of committed Visa/MasterCard jurors seemingly getting ready to assault jurors who were holding out for the merchants. When this happened, we walked into the jury deliberation room, stopped the escalating argument, thanked this panel of jurors and sent them home.

The jurors had been told that their videotaped deliberations and verdicts would help to shape the real trial. During the deliberations, several jurors speculated that their opinions might force the parties to settle the case, which they recognized would likely be a historic one. It was clear that the jurors had no idea whether Visa/MasterCard or the merchants were staging the mock trial. They liked certain witnesses and lawyers and hated others. Our economist, Frank Fisher, who testified live, was the witness the jurors respected most—even those who sympathized with the defendants.

Business executives and in-house lawyers from some of our giant merchant clients attended the simulations and watched four simultaneous deliberations through one-way glass and on split-screen closed-circuit televisions. The results of the trial simulations were less important than the exercise, which gave us the information needed to fine-tune our presentation. Nevertheless, the results were instructive. The one jury leaning toward Visa/MasterCard (8 to 2) was dismissed before blood was spilled. I was told by our trial consultants and psychologists that the strong feelings on that jury and other panels were an indication of the strength of the presentations and of the jurors' belief that the case was important to the country and to them as consumers.

The performance of the jury that was deadlocked and close to violence was particularly gratifying because they were one of two *struck* juries. The struck juries comprised jurors who had been surreptitiously dismissed by the plaintiffs, using "peremptory" and "for cause" challenges during the *voir dire*. This struck jury was primarily composed of jurors who we believed would be sympathetic to the defendants' arguments. In an actual jury selection, we would have overtly exercised our right to dismiss these jurors, most likely using peremptory challenges. Their demonstrated commitment to the defendants during the deliberations confirmed our judgments and the predictive value of the "good" and "bad" juror profiles we were using with the aid of jury specialists, public opinion pollsters and psychologists.

The other seven juries in the two trial simulations held in 2003 found for the merchants on the tying claim. Six of these juries also found for the merchants on the attempt-to-monopolize claim. Among the seven juries that reached a verdict, most but not all awarded damages in the billions. There was a lot of discussion in all of the juries about whether awarding damages to the merchants was fair, because the merchants and their expert, Dr. Fisher, had clearly told the jurors that the merchants were forced to charge shoppers higher prices as a result of the defendants' practices. One jury that found liability refused to award damages. I was glad that two of the eight juries gave us something to worry about and work on as we refined the case in the six weeks before trial. During that month, I watched the videotaped trial simulations over and over again and watched the deliberations of each of the eight juries twice. My written impressions of the simulations, added to consultants' evaluations and a poll conducted by yet another consultant, led to further refinements in our trial plan and in my opening statement.

My closing argument had sealed the deal at the March 2003 mock trial. At each trial simulation, I ended my closing argument by showing and quoting from a 1987 document where MasterCard angrily lashed out at Visa and Booz Allen Hamilton (BAH), a consulting firm that was advising both associations on their joint debit card strategy. Back then, discussing the exact same Visa/MasterCard conduct, which later would form the core of the Merchants' case, MasterCard contrasted what it and Visa had been able to get away with in the United States with the angry merchant backlash in the United Kingdom when Visa and its partner, Barclays Bank, had tried to do the same thing to U.K. merchants:

> **"If BAH really wanted to see what will likely happen on such a large scale they need only look to the United Kingdom where the merchant resistance caused Barclays to distinguish between debit and credit at the point of sale and price them differently. Additionally, that's exactly what will happen were we to try it anywhere else in Europe or Canada. We have been able to get away with it in America...."**

The MasterCard document then accurately predicted, *"We should point out that this matter will likely go to the courts...."* My closing argument always ended with this incredible document, and my plea: "Don't let them get away with it in America anymore." This closing primal scream visibly moved each jury. That was my powerful closing. But my opening statement was much too long and too complicated. Gene Cerruti, a law professor and friend whom we had hired to help with evidence issues, called my opening "Lloyd's Version of Shock and Awe." I constantly refined and shortened the opening statement during those last six weeks and constantly demanded that an audience critique each successive version. My opening was going to set the tone for the trial, and everybody had to be on board and to refine their own parts to harmonize with the promises I made to the jury at the beginning of trial. We were working 18-hour days, seven days a week until the last ten days before trial. Then the distinction between night and day lost any significance. The team would have been happy to just refine, polish and prepare until the morning of April 28, 2003, but for the April 1 summary judgment decision. That decision forced us to joyfully rework the entire trial script and my opening statement. We had to remove most of the evidence needed to prove the parts of the case that Judge Gleeson had just awarded us on the basis of his summary judgment decision. Judge Gleeson's decision also gave a jolt to what until then had been pro forma and futile settlement negotiations.

Breaking the Deadlock

THE MERCHANTS' CASE was very unlikely to settle before trial. I was firmly convinced of this from the earliest stages of the case in 1996, and I know that Visa's counsel shared my conviction. The case wouldn't settle because something more important than money was at stake. Visa and MasterCard's Honor All Cards rules, which required merchants that accepted one type of card to accept them all, was a fundamental business practice for both bank associations. Their arrangements for tying debit card acceptance to credit card acceptance were the foundation of their business models in the past as well as the basis of their plans for the future.

As joint ventures owned by nearly all (and all the same) U.S. banks, Visa/MasterCard operated as a bank cartel that had monopoly power in the credit card market. Using the Honor All Cards policies, Visa and MasterCard used their monopoly power to dominate the newer debit card market—amounting to hundreds of billions of dollars in annual transactions and projected to soon be a bigger market than credit cards. And if other types of payment cards had emerged, Visa and MasterCard would have enforced Honor All Cards to extend their monopoly into those markets as well.

At stake for Visa and MasterCard in the Merchants' case then was not just so many dollars in damages but the lynchpin of their business strategy. Larry Popofsky, Visa's lead counsel, stated at the very first court hearing that it was "probably a waste of the court's time" to try to get the parties to settle anytime before the summary judgment motions were decided. That did not occur until more than six years later.

The discovery in our case showed numerous analyses done by and for Visa that stressed that the tying arrangement was to be defended at all costs. One of these was The Shark. Another listed numerous concessions that could be made to end the litigation without eliminating the tying arrangement. That Visa analysis stressed that ending Honor All Cards was not something that could be agreed to. I knew that only two scenarios would force Visa and MasterCard to give up these policies. They would do this under court order or in the face of extinction. Conjure the late Charlton Heston vowing that the only way to take his gun would be "from my cold dead hands," and you get some sense of Visa and MasterCard's emotional attachment to these rules.

My conviction that the case would go to trial was based not only on the importance of the tying arrangements to the defendants, but also on my own needs and desires. I needed to believe that the case would not settle in order to get myself and my team to work hard enough to win. I wanted to try this case. I had envisioned a great trial from day one. Although the case took many different turns during its long course, everything that occurred confirmed and reinforced that image for me. The "rather theatrical" summary judgment hearing on January 10, 2003, in a "standing room only" courtroom, was a good preview of the glorious trial I had already played out in my mind. Our mock trials produced a fascinating clash of evidence, ideas and values, inciting some jurors to nearly assault one another and to treat certain lawyers like rock stars. These were good rehearsals. The paradox, of course, is that when you work so hard and so well that you are likely to win at trial, you force your adversary to capitulate and never get to actually try the case.

A Rough Start

On both sides sat experienced counsel. In some screened-off part of our brains, we all knew that the case might settle. One reason that settlement was conceivable involved MasterCard, the weak sister. Visa was way ahead of MasterCard in credit cards at the start of the case. Visa was even farther ahead in debit cards. Its lead in debit was so big that there was practically no second. So, while Visa and MasterCard were joined at the hip, MasterCard's share of the glory and money was relatively small. A smart and independent MasterCard would have settled the case in 1997 or 1998 by agreeing to abandon the tying arrangement in return for not paying damages. Such a settlement would likely have forced Visa to settle as well. MasterCard could then have competed in the rapidly expanding debit market with a fresh start on a substantially leveled playing field.

MasterCard either was not smart enough to understand this or insufficiently independent to do it, even if it understood. Nevertheless, beginning in 1997, Kevin Arquit, the head of Clifford Chance's antitrust practice and counsel for MasterCard, periodically had lunch with me in order to keep the lines of communication open. He and I knew that this would facilitate settlement, if discussions ever became serious. No lunches were necessary with Visa's counsel. There was longstanding mutual respect between me and Visa's attorneys Larry Popofsky and Steve Bomse, which could be tapped if necessary. Even so, I had drinks and breakfast with Popofsky every so often. In November 2001, after the Second Circuit affirmed Judge Gleeson's certification of the class, Popofsky called to congratulate me. During the call, we expressed our mutual admiration and realization that settlement discussions might eventually occur.

Settlement discussions are confidential and may not be revealed, even after settlement, except by mutual consent or court order. Therefore, I am severely limited in what I can say about the substance of the settlement discussions. I can say that a series of meetings with Visa took place in early 2002. They were futile except to confirm Magistrate Judge Mann's opinion, expressed at the conclusion of her settlement conference over two years earlier. She had said that the parties were so far apart that until something changed, further discussions were a waste of time. Nothing narrowed this gap in these early 2002 meetings. However, as the case headed towards trial, the possibility of mediation was discussed.

One early settlement meeting took place on February 13, 2002, but something that was *not* said that day wound up derailing the process for several months. What Visa's lawyers didn't tell me was that they were going to try to get another delay in the case by seeking an extension beyond the March 4, 2002, deadline to file their petition for *certiorari* in the United States Supreme Court. Such an extension would likely delay a ruling otherwise expected from the High Court in June until its October term, another long delay. The defendants hired Carter Philips of Sidley & Austin to handle the petition for certiorari.

Philips is one of a small group of Supreme Court specialists—a group that includes Ted Olson, Larry Tribe at Harvard, Walter Dellinger of O'Melveny & Myers and used to include (now Chief Justice) John Roberts when he was in private practice. These so-called Cert. Doctors have a way with the High Court. They typically are former clerks of the Justices and have made many appearances before the Court. They are likely to get courtesies from the Court that are not generally afforded to other lawyers who practice before it only occasionally, as I have. In Visa's case, Philips requested and was granted an extension by Justice Ginsburg before we had a chance to oppose it. Justice Ginsberg is the "Circuit Justice" assigned to rule on such procedural requests arising from cases in the Second Circuit. The request—served on C&P by *regular mail*—reached us six days after Justice Ginsburg had granted the extension. The extension would have prolonged the case by five months, instead of one, had we not hustled to file our briefs very early. That resulted in a denial of *certiorari* in June 2002, on one of the last days of the Court's term, instead of sometime during its next.

Settlement discussions require respect, civility and courtesy. Heller Ehrman's failure to tell me they would seek the delay and the regular-mail tactic used by their cocounsel at Sidley & Austin were breaches of professional courtesy and marked departures from the way the lawyers had behaved toward each other until that time.

After we feverishly prepared our expedited opposition to the defendants' petition to the Supreme Court, I traveled to Brussels with my younger daughter, Elizabeth, to give a speech about our case at a conference of European bankers. With the defendants' recent sleight of hand fresh in my sleep-deprived mind, I wrote, and rehearsed to Elizabeth, an extremely aggressive speech on the high-speed train trip between Paris and Brussels. I got our paralegal Jason Lipton to provide me with a visual aid for the speech. Projected on a large screen behind me, as I spoke to the bankers, was an image from Kaspar Meglinger's "Dance of Death" mural on the Spreuer Bridge in Lucerne. This mural commemorates the Black Plague by depicting skeletons dancing gaily in a circle. In comparing Visa and MasterCard's predicament to the victims of the Black Death in medieval Europe, I was, theatrically, underlining my predictions.

I predicted that (1) the Supreme Court would deny the bank associations' pending March 2002 request for a hearing, (2) the banks would be big losers, and the merchants big winners, when Judge Gleeson finally decided the pending summary judgment motions and (3) by then, potential damages would be so high for Visa and MasterCard that a trial would represent a bet-the-business contest against tough odds. A year after this April 2002 speech, when all the things I predicted had happened, MasterCard's CEO, Bob Selander, explained the settlement this way:

> "What happened with the retailers' suit is that we got caught in a situation where we were facing a trial and where the destiny of our company was going to be taken out of the hands of our board and shareholders and put in the hands of a jury. I don't think it is reasonable…to take a chance on losing control of your company to a jury verdict."

But at the time of my Brussels speech, a year earlier, the defendants considered my predictions impertinent and my "Dance of Death" imagery beyond the pale. Visa cancelled our next scheduled settlement meeting and called a halt, at least temporarily, to any further discussions.

The Cocksure Lawyer

An op-ed piece, titled "Wal-Mart's Ugly Suit," by James Glassman, appeared in the May 30, 2002, *Wall Street Journal* and alluded to the skeletons in my "Dance of Death" speech. Glassman is a frequently deployed right-wing pundit. He is the author of *Dow 36,000: The New Strategy for Profiting from the Coming Rise in the Stock Market*, a book written during the "irrational exuberance" of the Internet bubble. Glassman's op-ed attacked Wal-Mart and me by name. He wrote that my prediction that the Supreme Court would turn down Visa/MasterCard's petition for a hearing—much less grant a reversal of class certification—showed that, unless I "had tapped the Justices' chambers," I was just another "cocksure lawyer."

I consider assaults from the likes of Glassman, George Priest of Yale and Lester Brickman of Cardozo Law School, who also attacked our case in the media, to be badges of honor. However, the Glassman article either caused a fresh problem for Wal-Mart or exacerbated an existing one. Wal-Mart may have read the op-ed and felt that my in-your-face speech had provoked an attack on them in an influential newspaper. Wal-Mart heard a war cry for banks to close ranks and keep it from entering the financial services market, something it had long wanted to do.

Glassman's article took aim at Wal-Mart's attempt to buy the Franklin Bank in California. He speculated about the various ways Wal-Mart could use Franklin to enter the financial services market and lower credit card and debit card costs. At the time, the *American Banker* frequently published articles reflecting banks' fears about Wal-Mart. The Arkansas giant was an outsider already putting pressure on Visa and MasterCard. It might try competing directly with retail banks. Wal-Mart's historically successful low-cost/low-pricing strategy was anathema to the banks, which were using Visa/MasterCard to overcharge consumers. Wal-Mart may have thought that the Merchants' case, widely referred to in the media as "The Wal-Mart Suit," could impede the Franklin deal or that the Glassman article would stir up bank opposition to this proposed acquisition. Either way, Wal-Mart was angry, and it expressed its displeasure at a time when new leadership on the so-called Wal-Mart Legal Team was taking control.

Stung by a series of judicial rebukes and sanctions for allegedly failing to maintain or produce evidence in numerous cases, Wal-Mart had wisely made significant changes to its in-house counsel staff. Their choices for new leadership were generally good. At the very top, they brought in Tom Hyde, a sophisticated lawyer who had been Raytheon's General Counsel. However, they also hired Tom Mars for the number-two job and the title of being General Counsel of the world's largest business. Mars had been a partner in a Fayetteville firm, and before that he had been head of the Arkansas State Police.

The General Counsel's office at Wal-Mart began to pick fights with me, firing off memos demanding that I answer questions about the case, which the in-house Wal-Mart lawyers could have easily addressed. The most insulting was a question suggesting that C&P's contingency-fee arrangement created a conflict of interest, because we wanted to win big bucks, but it was in Wal-Mart's best interests to procure a speedy end to Visa and MasterCard's tying arrangements.

I sent back a wad of correspondence from 1996, documenting the genesis of the fee arrangement, including correspondence where I had advised Wal-Mart that the most important relief would be to end the tying arrangements and that any contingency fee should factor in the savings Wal-Mart realized from that result. I documented Wal-Mart's rejection of that proposal. Seeing how wrong and unprepared they were to argue with me just angered them more. Tom Mars "ordered" me to travel to Bentonville for a meeting with him on June 11, 2002.

On June 10, the day before my trip to Arkansas, the Supreme Court denied the defendants' petition for *certiorari*, ending their attempt to overturn Judge Gleeson's certification of a five million–member class. This was a day we had worked hard to achieve for more than three years. Our team and all of the other clients were jubilant. I received calls from numerous retailer CEOs and general counsel from around the country congratulating me and my firm for staying the course.

I awoke at 3:45 AM the morning of June 11, 2002, to catch the 6:00 AM flight to Bentonville. During the trip, I read the *New York Times'* and *Wall Street Journal's* coverage of the Supreme Court action. The *Journal*'s piece ran my pixilated headshot, which coincidentally was next to Eliot Spitzer's for a different article, which in turn was next to Manhattan District Attorney Bob Morgenthau's. Eliot and I have framed copies of this coincidence, the only time he was ever shown sandwiched between his two mentors. A few hours later in Bentonville, the article with my picture made my welcome even chillier than it had been intended to be.

Seated in the "Quail Room," the windowless space decorated with hunting photos of the late Sam Walton, was a group of grim-faced lawyers and a copy of the *Wall Street Journal* article spread out on the conference table. Tom Mars, who had ordered me to meet with him in Bentonville, was not in attendance.

The first thing said to me by one of the lawyers was, "I guess congratulations are in order. Now that *you* have *your* class, what are *you* going to do with it?" That was the worst moment in the entire case for me. To know that at a moment of victory, won after years of incredibly difficult team effort, our client was rooting against us, and against itself, was deeply depressing. I answered by congratulating *them* and telling *them* I was going to win "*their*" case, a case *they* had hired me to win. Readers who are familiar with what the leader of the Passover Seder says in response to the hostile question posed by the "wicked son" will immediately realize that my response to the Wal-Mart lawyer was loosely plagiarized from the Haggadah.

I demanded that Martin Gilbert, the Wal-Mart in-house lawyer who had negotiated the fee arrangement, come to the Quail Room. When Gilbert arrived, we reviewed the genesis of the fee arrangement. He confirmed everything that I had said and then left. I told the remaining lawyers that they could pull out of the case anytime they wanted. However, because Wal-Mart was a class representative, any separate deal it cut with the defendants would have to be submitted to Judge Gleeson for approval. The smarter lawyers around the table knew that this fight was over. I left Bentonville a lot happier than when I arrived, mulling the scene from *Butch Cassidy and the Sundance Kid*, where Cassidy (played by Paul Newman) is challenged to a fight a man twice his size and preempts the contest with a quick kick to the groin.

Wal-Mart hired Bernie Nussbaum of Wachtell Lipton to advise them about their prerogatives. Nussbaum had been President Clinton's counsel and Hillary Clinton's boss in the Watergate inquiry. (Hillary had been Tom Mar's boss at the Rose Law Firm in Arkansas.) Bernie has the ability and maturity to handle the most difficult legal problems and has made a career of doing it skillfully. I met with Nussbaum many times. We became friends and mutual admirers. Bernie told Wal-Mart that it was being well represented. Given the Wal-Mart approach to "buying" legal services, which were treated like a commodity, they needed the sage advice of lawyers like Nussbaum and his partner Meyer Koplow. To his credit, Tom Hyde must have recognized this when he retained Bernie. After a few nasty months, the Wal-Mart Legal Team began to behave. Wal-Mart's business executives had always been committed to the Merchants' case, and that commitment never wavered.

Buying Time

The Supreme Court's denial of *certiorari* may have initially depressed the lawyers at Wal-Mart, but it sobered Visa. Soon after, Larry Popofsky and I had lunch at the economics conference annually held by NERA in Santa Fe, where he forgave me for the Dance of Death speech. It is always gratifying to be forgiven for accurate predictions. My wife, Jan, then General Counsel of Rupert Murdoch's News America, occasionally used economists from NERA as experts in her cases. She and Popofsky were both attending the conference as NERA clients. The conference featured a presentation by Heller Ehrman lawyers about how to disqualify opposing economists with Heller Ehrman's *Daubert* motion tactics. I was there merely as a spouse, not a conference participant, but was well-known as the conference's former main speaker. As a guest, I was free to attend any session and chose to drop in at Heller Ehrman's *Daubert* session while it was in progress. The cognoscenti present giggled when they saw me enter the room. It was well known (in the small circle of elite antitrust lawyers and economists) that Heller Ehrman's *Daubert* gambit had backfired so badly that it not only failed to disqualify our economist, Professor Dennis Carlton, but had also resulted in NERA's star, Dean Richard Schmalensee, getting the boot from his lucrative and glamorous assignment in the Merchants' case.

I was also forgiven by Visa's Steve Bomse when we returned to court on June 21, 2002. The interrupted discussion about hiring a mediator resumed in July, and MasterCard was invited to join in the discussion. After months of swapping lists of potential mediators and interviewing a group of eminent candidates, which included a former Second Circuit judge and a former chairman of the Federal Trade Commission, we agreed to hire Boston University law professor Eric Green. Green was one of the two best-known mediators. Ken Feinberg, the head of the 9/11 Victims Compensation Fund, was the other one. He had more important things to do.

A month before Judge Gleeson's summary judgment decision, in March 2003, Magistrate Judge Mann summoned the parties for another settlement conference. I believe it was Mann's intention again to try her hand at forging a settlement. As the conference began, Mann asked whether any talks were taking place. Prior to the conference, the opposing parties had agreed not to reveal that we were engaged in a mediation process. But when asked the question directly, Bomse, Gallo, Arquit and I looked at each other and nodded, and one of us responded that Eric Green had been hired as our mediator.

One reason for breaking our vow of silence was to tell the truth. Another was to avoid an awkward confession to the magistrate judge, "We have agreed not to tell you." In my mind, there was a third and more important reason: I didn't want Magistrate Judge Mann's help. The manner in which she had conducted the earlier, December 1999, settlement conference and "supervised" the out-of-control process of discovery gave me little reason to want her assistance in further discussions. A name like Eric Green's was likely to get her to back off. And she did.

Eric Green is very good at what he does. But he needs parties who are willing to compromise their positions in order to conduct meaningful mediation sessions. At the time, Green didn't have the ingredients he needed. We had a lot of meetings, some with all of the parties together, but most with one side or the other meeting separately with Green. During these sessions, Green acted as a shuttle diplomat. The meetings and the preparations for them consumed precious time in the run-up to trial. We had none to waste, so we initially treated these sessions as additional prep sessions for the January 10, 2003, summary judgment argument. After that hearing, we used the meetings with Green as an opportunity to perform parts of our intended trial presentation.

We introduced Green to business executives and experts who summarized their likely trial testimony. We also tested video, trial graphics and documents. If Green was impressed by the strength of our case, he never showed it. Presumably, he was as poker-faced with Visa and MasterCard. To a mediator, who likes to stress the strengths of the other side, confidence from either party impedes settlement. Both sides exuded it, with the bank associations construing Judge Gleeson's admonitions, after the January 10, 2003 hearing, as a warning to the merchants. We construed the same words as a warning to Visa/MasterCard. Green's skeptical, almost amused attitude never wavered—except on the night of April 1, when he called me saying he guessed I was right about whom Judge Gleeson had threatened on January 10. I had admired Green's acting skills, which are so important to a mediator's craft. His terse admission on that April Fool's night was clearly a studied response. Had he failed to acknowledge the significance of Gleeson's decision, I would have lost respect for his acting skills.

Until April 1, 2003, the mediation was going nowhere. Then Judge Gleeson's seismic summary judgment decision, so completely in our favor, made things look bleak for Visa and MasterCard. It gave Eric Green what he needed. But Green also needed to push back against any belief on our part that the case was already over. Although the liability case was more or less won, the trial simulations convinced us that the issue of damages was more than a tap-in.

Real settlement discussions with both Visa and MasterCard began the day after the summary judgment decision in April 2003. The parties gave Eric Green permission to bring in a second mediator, Jonathan Marks. He was the same lawyer who assisted Green in the mediation toward the end of the *Microsoft* antitrust case. Green said that the number of meetings necessary to fully explore settlement could not be handled by a single mediator. Bringing in Marks raised the price of the daily mediation fee to $20,000.

In his April 1, 2003, summary judgment decision, Judge Gleeson delivered on what he had previously called a "strongly, strongly" put warning to settle before he issued the summary judgment decision. He ordered the parties to appear in his chambers on April 9 and began to tighten the screws. I won't reveal what was said on that day. However, the tactics used by Judge Gleeson can be revealed. They were simple, forceful and effective. He deprived us, and especially me, of time to make the countless last-minute preparations for trial. I was plaintiffs' lead trial counsel, and my opening statement would begin the trial. Perhaps more wisely, the defendants used one set of lawyers to discuss settlement and another to serve as lead trial counsel.

Our case, which went first, had to be substantially reformatted after the summary judgment decision. Because Judge Gleeson had eliminated most of the liability case, the opening, which I had worked on for months, had to be completely redone. All of the live testimony had to be changed. All of the defendants' and third parties' video depositions had to be re-edited. All of the questions and answers designed to prove that there were a credit card market and a debit card market, that credit and debit cards were distinct products, that the two products had been tied, and that Visa had market power as well as others—all of this had to be eliminated. Judge Gleeson would simply instruct the jury that these things had already been determined. He would not allow us to waste his or the jury's time on any of this. Scaling back our case, however propitious, would require enormous amounts of time. Judge Gleeson was depriving me of this vital time. As a former trial lawyer, Gleeson knew exactly what he was doing to me. But in case he had forgotten, I reminded him. I only did this once, however, because afterward he made things worse for me.

Judge Gleeson pointedly and repeatedly told me and my clients that if we didn't settle we would "still get a fair trial," a phrase that by its sheer superfluity acts as a kind of doublespeak. Every lawyer assumes a fair trial. When a judge keeps insisting that you're going to get one, it's an implicit threat that maybe you won't, that various things will be made very difficult for you. This statement became more threatening each time Gleeson repeated it. Given the prerogatives of a trial judge and his extraordinarily wide latitude to decide what constituted a "fair" trial, the lawyers were confused and nervous about what the judge meant. Judge Gleeson sensed this uncertainty and exploited it. I also believed, and constantly reminded my clients, that Judge Gleeson was issuing similar warnings to the defendants, though likely much harsher. After all, he had just flattened them at summary judgment and put us in the driver's seat.

On April 10, the day after the first post-summary judgment meeting with Judge Gleeson, Kevin Arquit and I had a cup of coffee at the Doubletree Hotel on Lexington Avenue and 51st Street. I left our brief meeting reasonably sure that MasterCard was throwing in the towel. I can't overstate the difficulty of that moment for me. There had been and would be worse, but this one was very difficult because of the psychological and logistical problems it created.

Although I was reasonably sure that MasterCard was surrendering, I was not positive. If they did, Visa would likely have to follow suit, even if they were otherwise inclined to risk the Dance of Death. Having been through this many times before (albeit never in a case nearly as large), I knew that the settlement, if it occurred, would come no earlier than the day before trial. The "day before" or "day of trial" settlement is so typical that it seems to be a "constant," like the speed of light in physics. That is what happened in 1998 in our antitrust case against AOL and in 2001 in our antitrust case against Time Warner and in a bunch of other cases along the way. With all this in my mind, I feared that we would kill ourselves to reformat the Merchants' case, because of Judge Gleeson's summary judgment decision, and still never get to use the beautiful opening, the skillful direct and cross examinations and the thousand other elegant trial presentations we had painstakingly created.

I had to avoid a letdown and be ready to try the case. I had to hide the likelihood of settlement from all but the absolute minimum number of people. Most of our trial team were told that the settlement discussions were pro forma and likely futile. They believed this was true because we all did until April 1 and because they, as much as I, wanted it to be true and to have our trial. The mock trials and the summary judgment hearing had put everyone on our side in a state of great excitement. They needed to stay that way, and I needed to compartmentalize my brain and keep half in that trial-ready state.

Commencing three weeks before trial, there were live meetings or teleconferences with the mediators every day. Judge Gleeson had ordered the parties to return to his chambers on April 14, this time with the mediators. At that meeting, he increased the pressure and ordered the mediators and parties to give him a daily progress report.

Judge Gleeson ordered us into chambers again on April 22 and that day issued an order for executives at the CEO or CFO levels of Visa, MasterCard, Wal-Mart, Sears, The Limited, Safeway, Circuit City, The National Retail Federation, The Food Marketing Institute and The International Mass Retail Association to come to Brooklyn and be prepared to stay in negotiations until either a settlement was reached or the trial began six days later. I referred to this forced stay of the executives in Brooklyn as the "Days of Incarceration."

Over the years, my desire to be a federal judge has vacillated, peaking twice before that moment in the Merchants' case. The first time was early in my career after watching District Judge Jack Weinstein at work, helping humanity by being a tough and brilliant dude. The second time was in 1992 during a brief moment of delusional euphoria, when I expected that Bob Abrams would become a United States Senator and deliver on a promise made to me during his campaign. After Bob lost the election to the incumbent Al D'Amato, I lost interest in a federal judgeship until April 2003. During one of Judge Gleeson's round-the-clock sessions in Brooklyn at the United States Courthouse, I told him that what he was doing to me had rekindled my interest in being a federal judge. I said, "Some day, I want to be able to do to some other poor bastard, what you are doing to me now."

Preparing for the January 2003 summary judgment hearing, I believed that Judge Gleeson would be more offended by proof that Visa and MasterCard had knowingly harmed consumers and small store owners than by evidence that they had intentionally violated the antitrust laws. Sensing this, I ended my summary judgment argument with a document accurately painting that harsh picture of Visa. Gleeson's April 1 summary judgment decision was devastating to both defendants but especially tough on Visa.

During the days of incarceration in late April 2003, I again got to see how right I was about Judge Gleeson's populist tendencies. He was going to imprison the highly paid senior business executives and general counsel of my five giant retailer clients until they acted responsibly. He viewed them as overpaid, spoiled high rollers working for mega merchants whose class action was, as he would later tell us, "riding on the backs of the small store owners of America." He lectured to them, "You have won this case," and advised them to settle for the billions of dollars being offered but, more importantly, for the injunctive relief that included an end to Visa and MasterCard's Honor All Cards tying arrangements. This was the core of the case, and the relief most likely to help those millions of small store owners and hundreds of millions of American consumers.

If motivating my clients to settle required keeping them over the weekend in a tiny witness room that stank of takeout food and backed-up toilets, even better. Gleeson wouldn't allow the executives to leave, even for emergencies. One was permitted to go home only when a new hostage arrived from a thousand miles away to replace her. I stupidly took a chance and allowed one high-level executive to leave without Judge Gleeson's permission and was subsequently tongue-lashed and nearly held in contempt of court for doing so.

The incarceration put more pressure on me than it did on my clients. I needed to prepare for trial. I also felt responsible for these client-warriors, who included Steve Cannon and Linda English from Circuit City; Bob Gordon and Dennis Stokely from Safeway; Chris Crow, Carol Ann Petren, Ellenore Angelidis and Glenn Richter from Sears; Jay Fitzsimmons, Mike Cook and Ross Higman from Wal-Mart; Mike Canter and Lisa Klinger from The Limited; Mallory Duncan and Tracy Mullin from NRF; George Green from FMI; Moe Cain and Sandy Kennedy from IMRA; and others who came and went as part of Judge Gleeson's hostage-exchange program. They never complained and managed to adopt a spirited boot camp mentality. They did everything in their power to keep me going, knowing I was exhausted and that my private shuttle diplomacy sessions with the Judge were rough and highly charged. The parties had consented to Judge Gleeson holding these private sessions with each side, as if we really had any choice but to consent to the judge who was about to conduct his "fair trial." In the meantime, Judge Gleeson was also skillfully using the mediators to deliver veiled threats and engage in a kind of legal hazing. Still, I did not want to settle. Winning was not enough for me, I wanted my trial.

Letting Go

I had worked toward this moment for 12 years and didn't want to win my Wimbledon on what would feel like a default. In resisting Judge Gleeson's demand that we take our victory and do the right thing for the small stores, I tried to hide behind my huge retailer clients. I told Judge Gleeson that I could not force these big guys to settle. After all, I was just their lawyer. He responded, "This is your case. You are counsel for the entire class and have a responsibility to all of them. You can settle this case even without the consent of any of the five big stores."

I told Judge Gleeson I knew that he was technically correct, but after their years of expensive, noble and unselfish service as champions for the class, I probably would not settle without their consensus approval. Instead, I would convince them to settle, but only if I was convinced that it was the right thing to do. My heart said it was wrong to settle, but my brain said it was right. So, I convinced them. But it was very painful and took not hours or days but six weeks.

My clients agreed to settle in three stages. The first was on my "verbal handshake" with MasterCard at 4:45 AM on April 28, 2003, while I was lying on a king-sized bed with Bob Begleiter, Mitch Shapiro and George Sampson in the Marriott Hotel in downtown Brooklyn. Later that morning, we picked the jury, and I was scheduled to give my opening argument. The second stage was when we signed written memoranda of understanding with both Visa and MasterCard on the evening of April 30 in the offices of Simpson Thacher, a firm brought in by MasterCard toward the end of the case. This came after the trial team, for the second time, completely reformatted the case, this time for a trial against Visa only. They did this in only 60 hours.

The third-stage final settlements were long, detailed and heavily negotiated documents. They are dated June 4, 2003, but were actually signed on June 5, at 5:30 AM in C&P's midtown office. After I signed them, I went directly to play squash and after that to a long-deferred appointment with a podiatrist at the Hospital for Special Surgery. He took one look at me, told me I was dangerously dehydrated, and instead of treating my injured foot, sent me to my internist, Larry Inra, who immediately sent me to a gastroenterologist, Paul Miskovitz, who put me on medication for dehydration, which had been worsening for months. Two weeks after the January 2003 summary judgment hearing, my exhaustion and dehydration caused me to lock up at the midtown Marriott Marquis Hotel, where I was chairing a panel on "Antitrust Federalism—the clash between federal and state enforcement." The speakers, including Debbie Majoras, later

"Chairman" of the FTC and Eliot Spitzer, then New York's Attorney General, asked me why I wouldn't sit down. I lied and claimed nervousness. Marty Jaramillo, the chief physical therapist at the Hospital for Special Surgery was dispatched, met me in a hotel room, massaged me until I could bend and got me to drink two quarts of salty liquids. Nevertheless, the condition persisted for months. On June 5, the gastroenterologist ordered me not to travel to Australia as I was scheduled to later that week. He said the long flight would seriously exacerbate my severe dehydration. I complied and waited a few days to follow Jan and see our "baby," Elizabeth, who was in Tasmania as an exchange student. When I returned to the U.S. and had my deferred visit with Dr. Rock Positano, the foot guy, he confirmed what the gastroenterologist had told me—had I taken the 20-plus-hour direct flight to Sydney, Australia, without being treated for dehydration, I might have died.

While all this was happening, I thought about a five-set third-round match I had attended between Jim Courier and Sjeng Schalken at Wimbledon in 1999. After the conclusion of the fifth set, which Courier won 13–11, both players were taken to the hospital and treated for dehydration. I was one of the few Americans to watch the entire match on a small and intimate Wimbledon side court. All by myself, I matched the volume and intensity of a screaming bunch of face-painted Dutchmen rooting for Schalken. As Courier left the court to go to the hospital, he turned directly to me and thrust his clenched fist at me in victory and appreciation for my patriotic and rowdy support. As the doctor re-hydrated me on June 5, 2003, I thought of Jim Courier, clenched my fist and sent him telepathic thanks for giving me something to emulate.

Settlement

———

DURING THE EVENING of April 30, I accepted the fact that the case would settle. That night, the merchants, MasterCard and Visa signed short-form, but binding, memoranda of understanding containing the outlines of the Settlement. At that moment, I surrendered my plans for a beautiful trial. The next day, I settled my bill at the Brooklyn Marriott, where the weekend before, I had checked in for 92 days. Several circumstances delayed the depression that I eventually experienced. That night, the demons were warded off by sheer physical exhaustion and a comic incident.

I signed the MasterCard agreement early in the evening and the Visa agreement at 10:00 PM At about 10:15 PM, the lawyers for all the parties were summoned to a hearing by teleconference on a motion that Visa had just made. Visa was asking Judge Gleeson to lift the gag order he had imposed on the parties two days earlier.

After we had shaken hands with MasterCard, on April 28, Judge Gleeson had prohibited any party from publicly discussing the verbal MasterCard settlement, or the ongoing settlement negotiations involving Visa. This had been done to protect Visa, as much as possible, from the impact that MasterCard's billion-dollar-plus settlement might have on a jury who had been read a jury questionnaire telling them that the merchants of America were accusing Visa *and* MasterCard of engaging in an antitrust conspiracy. The jury might infer Visa's culpability from MasterCard's settlement and its payment of such a large sum of money.

Someone had leaked the MasterCard settlement to the press. An article describing the verbal settlement, with specifics that could only be known by an insider, appeared on the front page of the *Wall Street Journal* on April 29. My speculation is that MasterCard leaked their own settlement and that they did it in an effort to control the spin. If they leaked the story, and for that reason, the strategy failed. There's just no way to put a positive spin on more than a billion dollars, plus a massive price reduction and the surrender of a basic business practice that you have repeatedly told the press is a necessity for your business, is good for consumers and will be defended until the end of time.

Once the MasterCard settlement was leaked to the *Wall Street Journal*, articles appeared in hundreds of other media outlets on April 30. At some point that day, Visa released a statement in blatant violation of the gag order. Now Visa was asking Judge Gleeson to lift the gag order it had already violated. Coming at the very end of an incredibly tense month, this was not as funny as it sounds and Judge Gleeson was not amused. He ripped into Visa as they began to argue that they had violated the gag order only because they were sure that either the merchants or MasterCard must have violated it first. MasterCard's indignance, contrived or genuine, made the situation even worse. I just kept my mouth shut, which is as hard as it is rare for me.

After threatening contempt against Visa, Judge Gleeson pointed out that he had imposed the gag order for Visa's benefit. We all knew that Gleeson properly didn't like gag orders or any impediments to press and public scrutiny of his courtroom and proceedings. When Gleeson granted the *Wall Street Journal*'s motion to open up the files back in June 2002, he had gone well beyond the *Journal*'s request and unsealed virtually everything. On that night of April 30, 2003, Judge Gleeson kept the gag order in place only until the next morning to enable MasterCard to get their press office ready. They claimed to need this extra time. Our press consultant, Kent Jarrell, was ready and scheduled a news conference for the next morning.

The news conference proved to be a catharsis for me. I got to say precisely what I thought about the settlements and the process that had produced them, without time to edit, embellish, or rationalize. Here is most of what I was asked, and said, similarly unedited:

> LLOYD CONSTANTINE: "I am the managing partner of this law firm, Constantine & Partners—good name—and I'm lead counsel for the merchants in this litigation. And I'm happy to be joined by Bob Begleiter and George Sampson, my co-lead counsel. And all the people you see around me are the team that litigated this case, and they're the people who won this case.
>
> So, anyway, I'm glad to be here today, and I'll just make a brief opening statement. I didn't get to make my opening statement at the trial, so I'll make my brief opening statement now, and then I'll answer your questions.
>
> We're very happy today because we feel that we have achieved a great result for our clients, which are virtually every store in the United States, every merchant in the United States, and virtually every consumer in the United States. This was a case against Visa and MasterCard, which is a cartel of 8,000 banks. Visa and MasterCard are owned by the same banks, they're members of the same banks, and they do the same thing. And that's what this case was about.
>
> They imposed their regime of price-fixing and restraint of trade on merchants in America. They were forcing merchants

in the United States to take debit card transactions at credit card prices, they were denying merchants freedom of choice, and that imposed billions of dollars in extra cost on merchants every year. All those costs were passed along to consumers in the form of higher prices.

Beginning today, that is going to end almost immediately. As of May 1 of this year, merchants in the United States are being paid $50 million. Beginning on August 1 of this year, Visa and MasterCard prices and the prices of all of their banks are going to drop by more than a billion dollars to merchants just for the balance of this year, and that's going to lead to lower prices for American shoppers.

Beginning in 2004—on January 1, 2004, merchants in the United States will have a right that they never had before, which is to freely choose to accept certain Visa or MasterCard products or not, based upon their quality and based upon their price. They just never had that opportunity before. And for the first time, they will have the opportunity to purchase the use of these services in a free and open market. And that's going to lead to better products and lower prices for every store in the United States. We're very happy about that. We're very happy that the people who you see around you were able to deliver this result for every store in the United States and for every consumer in the United States. And it is an important achievement.

These people, this firm, and the other firms that assisted us went to battle with four of the finest and largest law firms in the world—Clifford Chance, Heller Ehrman, Simpson Thacher, and Arnold & Porter. And they were good, fine adversaries, but this group of people matched them and overmatched them on behalf of a very important cause—the cause of American consumers and American merchants where tens of millions—tens of millions of Americans work. And so we're very happy about that and very proud of our achievement.

And today is the beginning of a new day in the United States, where the system of free enterprise actually comes to Visa and MasterCard. And actually I think it's a good day for them, too, because I think ultimately they will not only survive in that system, but they will thrive because the wisdom of the antitrust laws is that people do better when they compete. Starting today, Visa and MasterCard will compete for the business of merchants, for the business of consumers, and they will compete with each other. That's a very important result. And this firm and all these people you see around me—we have some of our clients here from Sears Roebuck, as well, have worked really hard for this result. So, that's what I have to say, and I will answer your questions."

REPORTER: "Can you give us an example of how this might affect an individual store? I mean how the practice—what would the store have to pay, or the retailer have to pay, or the chain have to pay that it might not have had to pay?"

LLOYD CONSTANTINE: :It's very, very simple. On August 1 of this year, Visa and MasterCard are going to drop their fees by at least a third on a bunch of products which will be sold in the United States for more than $400 billion in transactions this year. So, more—there will be more than $400 billion in debit transactions this year, and the prices of all those debit transactions will drop by a third or even more on August 1."

REPORTER: "And what percentage of that $400 billion just represents the fee? I mean how much..."

LLOYD CONSTANTINE: "The fee is a percentage—usually somewhere between one-and-a-half percent and two percent of that transaction. That in and of itself amounts to billions of dollars a year.

For the rest of this decade, the court has estimated in a published decision that the value of the injunction that we won in this case is going to run between $63 billion and $100 billion in lower prices—lower costs to American stores, which is going to result in lower prices to American consumers. That's not just our calculation. That's a calculation of Federal District Judge John Gleeson and the Second Circuit Court of Appeals that the value of this injunction for the balance of the decade is worth somewhere between $63 and $100 billion. That's the real worth of what we've achieved.

You know, it was nice to get a few billion dollars in damages, and that was fine. But it's a much less significant result than what's going to happen in the future. When we began this case, there were $20 to $30 billion a year in these transactions. This year, there will be $400 billion. By the end of the decade, there'll be over a trillion dollars annually in these transactions.

So, the dimensions of this are getting greater and greater. The harm was getting greater and greater. Therefore, the benefit going forward will be greater and greater. And so, the real benefit of this is a better deal for merchants and a better deal for American consumers."

REPORTER: "Can you sort of walk us through how this deal came together in the last 24 hours? And what effect did the MasterCard settlement on Monday have on these talks?"

LLOYD CONSTANTINE: "I can barely walk, let alone walk you through it. (LAUGHTER)

It actually came together over the last week. And what happened in the last week—and I'm smiling now, but it was—it was a rough week. It was a rough week for everybody—for our clients, for our adversaries who are, you know, fine people, and for us here.

Around a week ago, Judge John Gleeson called all of the major parties into New York and asked them to seriously consider whether or not they should go to trial on this case with such high stakes because he believed there was a resolution and a compromise which would best serve the interests of all the parties and the American economy. And so, all of the top executives from Sears and Wal-Mart and Circuit City and Safeway and The Limited and The National Retail Federation and The Food Marketing Institute and The International Mass Retail Association on our side and Visa and MasterCard and many bank executives from Bank of America and Banc One and Chase and Citicorp all arrived in New York and began a series of very, very arduous shuttle negotiations supervised by the court.

And that went on for the entire week, including the entire weekend, late into the night well into the morning. Some of the people who are standing here were involved in that. Some of those negotiations took place here. Some took place at another law firm. Many of those took place right in the courthouse. Judge Gleeson essentially commandeered the courthouse, made available jury rooms and back rooms and his chambers and empty courtrooms to put all these various people in because there had to be lots of different conversations between groups of business people and lawyers and with the judge and without the judge, and that all took place literally on a 24-hour basis for the entire week.

And it was through that process—through that very painful process—both physically painful and emotionally painful—that the resolution in this case was hammered out. And I think everybody on all sides of this case owes a debt of gratitude to that judge because in my 31 years of practice, I have never seen a judge handle something on one level with such vigor but on another level with such intelligence. So, that's how it happened."

REPORTER: "...from CNN. If you could prove what your damages were—and I believe antitrust cases have settled at so many treble damages—why would you settle for only one or two billion when you can calculate damages way higher than that number?"

LLOYD CONSTANTINE: "If we could have proven our damage methodology, we would have wound up with a gazillion dollars, OK? And that gazillion dollars would have been like Confederate money—for a variety of reasons. One, there is no way that either of the associations had the ability to pay that. Two, they would have launched off on an appellate process, which would have taken up until 2007. We would have probably been up to the Supreme Court again. You know, we've already been to the Supreme Court on this case once. It took two-and-a-half years' delay.

So, we would have been in 2006 or 2007 before we would have seen any of that—any of that money. In the meantime, the injunction was the issue. In those two to three years, an additional $30 to $40 billion in real tangible damage would have been done to American stores and American consumers. And so, while it was nice to collect $3, $4 billion—that was, and that's what, we got. That paled in comparison—was so insignificant to stopping this—to stopping it right in its tracks.

The best thing that's happening right now is that on May 1, you know, we have stopped this. There will be great reductions on August 1. And our merchants will be free and American consumers will be free on January 1, 2004. That would have not have happened if we had won a trillion dollars times three.

The collectibility of that money was seriously in doubt, and we knew there was no doubt that that day would have been many years from now. And that is—that is one of the issues which the judge I think quite wisely impressed upon us, that you can have a paper judgment, but you will not get the injunctive relief which you can get right now [(inaudible)] he said, 'You have won this case."

REPORTER: "So, this settlement precludes merchants following up on their own then?"

LLOYD CONSTANTINE: "Well, going forward, merchants can do what they want. But in terms of the case that we filed on October 25, 1996, it is concluded. Now, it's not completely concluded. There's going to be a notification to five million merchants, which will be sent out. They will have an opportunity to say what they think about this—to object. And that—there's a process, and we honor that process.

So, five million merchants will get a notice, and they'll be able to say, "Lloyd, you didn't do a good enough job," if that's what they think. But we are very proud of what we've done. And I think that the people around here are proud of what we've achieved."

REPORTER: "What is the plan for dividing up the money among the retailers? And can you talk a little bit more about what the process is for getting this approved....?"

LLOYD CONSTANTINE: "Sure, sure. Again, and I think I can't stress enough how important the going-forward injunction is. But in terms of the few billion dollars that we're going to collect here, the plan is very simple.

Every merchant in the United States is treated exactly equally. The five merchants who originally brought the case, and then there were 12 additional smaller merchants who joined in, will get exactly—you know, according to the exact same formula—as every small, large, or medium-sized merchant in the United States. It is completely based upon their forced purchase of Visa and MasterCard off-line signature debit transactions.

So, if they've purchased, you know, a million dollars of those, they will get something based upon that purchase. If they've purchased $100,000 of those, they will get something based upon that. It will be directly proportional to the number of those transactions and the value of those transactions that were forced on them.

So, it's quite simple. Everybody gets treated equally. It's all subject to court approval. At the end of the day, the judge will sign off on it, so it will be his plan. Everything from this time on is the judge's plan. He has to approve everything. He has to protect the interests of those five million merchants. And he also sees very much his role in protecting American consumers in this case. I know that because he told it to us."

REPORTER: "What would you say was the toughest part of the agreement to reach?"

LLOYD CONSTANTINE: "I think the toughest part of the agreement on both sides, and I shouldn't speak for my adversaries, but it was surrendering and letting go, and we had to surrender, too. We had to surrender, you know, our vision of a wonderful trial, of a beautiful opening argument. All the people around me you see, have worked inhumane hours for years, absolutely—I mean, I have never seen a level of dedication like this, and I assume the same thing was happening on the other side. You fall in love with your direct examination of Ms. Jones or Mr. Smith. You fall in love with the perfect cross-examination that you've prepared for Carl Pascarella or Bob Selander. You fall in love with your opening argument, I'm going to keep my opening argument in a box, you know, the way Alexander the Great kept the Iliad in a box. I'm going to keep that in a box; I think mine is slightly better, but I'm going to do that.

And all of the people here have those things. To surrender that on behalf of your clients, on behalf of consumers, is a tough thing to do, so surrendering that has been the hardest part. On the other side, they had an almost religious fervor about some of their rules. They really truly believed in those rules, and they had to surrender that as well. So, the hardest part was not the physical torture which we went through, the hardest part was surrendering—it was the hardest part for me. In that respect, I think Judge Gleeson helped us."

REPORTER: "You mentioned the inhumane hours that you've been working back since 1996. How do you get compensated for those hours?"

LLOYD CONSTANTINE: We get compensated by Judge Gleeson. The way that you get compensated in a class action is that you submit a plan to the judge, who approves it. You make sure that it's fair and equitable, and he decides what you get paid. And I can tell you that right now that is the last thing on my mind.

The only reason that the people around here would work as hard as we've worked was for two reasons. One for the results; for our clients and for consumers. The other thing is for the work, for the joy of the work. It's hard, but it's joyful, and you cannot do it unless you have joy in it. So, some day down the line, we'll put together a fee application, Judge Gleeson will get it, he'll say whether we did a good job or a bad job, and we get paid what he says."

Books that recount an event from one person's perspective frequently resort to descriptions of the "worst moment," "best moment," "hardest thing," and other subjective reactions stated in the superlative. This book inevitably has its share. Here is the only moment, in this very long case, that made me cry. The proud father of one of C&P's lawyers attended the press conference. He forwarded a copy of the transcript to Paul Ward, a colleague of his who was a high-level aide to Cardinal Egan in the New York Archdiocese. Ward's reactions were passed along to me.

> "...I really appreciated Lloyd's comments about the need to 'surrender' in order to do something that makes sense or that is good. When you think about it spiritually, it's very Christ-like: 'whoever would save his life must lose it.'"

The tears shed after reading these comments helped this Jewish man reach emotional closure with the Settlement.

After that May 1, 2003, news conference, we began to work on a fully fleshed-out final Settlement, which was signed on June 5, 2003. The Settlement provided a bundle of very complicated and important injunctive relief for the merchants. But the simplest and most important provisions of the Settlement were the following seven, in the exact words and order of priority assigned to them in Judge Gleeson's December 19, 2003, decision approving the Settlement, followed by my bracketed explanations where necessary.

(1) "The cessation, as of January 1, 2004, of defendants' 'Honor All Cards' rules, by which the defendants' debit card services to merchants were tied to their credit card services." *[The tying arrangements cease]*

(2) "The creation of a $3.05 billion settlement fund." *[Paid by Visa/MasterCard.]*

(3) "The creation of clear conspicuous and uniform visual identifiers on Visa and MasterCard debit cards by January 1, 2007 (80% by July 1, 2005), so merchants and consumers can distinguish these products from credit cards." *[The reissuance or more than 250 million cards with the word "DEBIT" clearly and conspicuously placed directly above the Visa and MasterCard names. That new DEBIT identification on all future cards, already numbering over 500 million.]*

(4) "The lowering, by roughly one third, of the interchange rates on debit products for the period from August 1, 2003, through December 31, 2003." *[A price decrease to merchants in that brief period amounting to more than $1 billion and which continued beyond that period.]*

(5) "Other injunctive relief, such as the provision of signage from defendants to merchants communicating the merchants' acceptance of defendants' untied debit products; and a prohibition on defendants enacting any rules that prohibit merchants from encouraging or steering customers to use forms of payment other than defendants' debit cards, including by discounting other forms of payment." *[Visa and MasterCard had to make it easy for merchants to choose whether to continue accepting untied debit cards and credit cards and provide multiple notices and signage to ease this process. Visa and MasterCard had to stop preventing stores from urging their customers to use other forms of payment.]*

(6) "The Court's continuing jurisdiction to ensure compliance with the Settlement." *[The Court makes sure that all the relief that Visa and MasterCard agreed to provide is in fact provided. Court supervision continues today and will continue.]*

(7) "The release of Visa and MasterCard from claims arising out of the conduct at issue in the action prior to January 1, 2004." *[Visa and MasterCard must live up to their obligations under the Settlement, other than that their part of the Merchants' case is over. The Court and C&P (now Constantine Cannon) still have work to do and are still doing it.]*

Judge Gleeson's description of the core relief in the Settlement was concise and impeccable. I generally agree with his order of priority, believing that prohibiting the "Honor All Cards" tying arrangements was the most important relief. However, I would shift his number three to second place, because I also consider the redesign and replacement of more than 250 million debit cards (and billions of future cards) with clear, conspicuous and uniform debit identification to be more important than the cash payment of $3.05 billion, even though this was by far the largest monetary recovery in any federal antitrust case. Judge Gleeson found that the total present value of the compensatory relief recovered (including the immediate mandated price drop) was $3.383 billion, a figure that exceeded the compensatory relief in the previous eight highest federal antitrust class action recoveries, *combined*!

I believe that the redesign of the cards was more important than the money relief because the discovery had shown that, in addition to deceiving stores, the design of Visa/MasterCard debit cards to look like credit cards had caused massive harm to consumers. Shoppers frequently drained their checking accounts and bounced checks because they thought they were using a credit card. These incidents were little nightmares with collateral consequences that reverberated for weeks, months and, sometimes, for years. The jury would have heard the testimony of some of the victimized consumers, but it was better that the underlying cause of their problems was corrected. All of the cards were also electronically redesigned so that merchants can identify debit cards using codes embedded in the magnetic stripe on the cards.

The basic idea of American antitrust is that consumers, businesses and the economy, all do better with competitive markets than where there is little or no competition. Antitrust is not a regulatory scheme. Neo-conservatives who refer to government antitrust enforcers as "regulators" do so either ignorantly or maliciously. Being anti-regulatory, antitrust does not predict outcomes other than the broad prediction that more competition produces better results than less competition. Some critics of antitrust point to this imprecision to support their charge that antitrust is sort of a creed, if not a religion. That criticism has some but little merit. Those who heard or read what I said about antitrust and the results of the Merchants' case at the May 1, 2003, press conference may discern a little of the preacher in me.

Payday

JUDGE GLEESON ISSUED his fee decision on December 19, 2003, along with his approval of the Settlement. These are the facts about the fee award. We applied to Judge Gleeson for an attorneys' fee amounting to 18% of the present value of the monetary relief to the merchants, which Judge Gleeson determined was $3.383 billion. In fact, we underestimated the amount of the immediate negotiated price decrease, which actually added some $400 million to this $3.4 billion figure. Our request was also calculated as a percentage of the value of monetary relief and the injunctive relief, including the elimination of the tying arrangements, which is projected to range from $25 billion to $87 billion during just the first decade after the Settlement. So, as a percentage of the whole package of relief, quantified by Judge Gleeson in his decision, our request was as high as 2.14% to as low as 0.67%, or roughly two-thirds of one percent. The amount requested was identical in each of these three percentage calculations, $608,940,000.

In his decision, Judge Gleeson called our fee request "excessive" and "absurd" and "wholly out of character for a group of counsel whose commitment to the corner store merchants they represent has, until now, been admirable and unflagging." Judge Gleeson then awarded an attorneys' fee of $220,290,160.44. He said that the six factors that govern the award of attorneys' fees "compels the award of an extraordinary fee." The fee he awarded was the highest ever awarded in a federal antitrust case. Those are the facts, but not the truth, about the fee and the process that led up to Judge Gleeson's decision.

The truth is that Judge Gleeson, who otherwise did his job throughout the case skillfully and with great integrity, was disingenuous about his method in making this decision. It is silly and truly absurd to try to gain sympathy when you have been awarded a nine-figure attorneys' fee, the highest ever in this area of law. That's not my purpose. I simply want to go beyond the publicly known facts to the truth.

During the brutal settlement process, I got to know, like and respect John Gleeson. After we settled, I knew that Judge Gleeson would have a problem with the attorneys' fee. No matter how small a fee he awarded when measured as a percentage of the relief, it was inevitably going to be the largest fee in federal antitrust history, because the recovery was so much larger than any previous antitrust recovery. The previous record was $1.027 billion in the 1998 NAS-DAQ antitrust settlement. The merchants' compensatory relief, at $3.383 billion, was more than three times this previous record. Moreover, the injunctive relief, valued at $25 to $87 billion, which Judge Gleeson said "should inform my decision on awarding fees and it has," rendered comparison with any previous result almost impossible.

Knowing that the fee would likely be the largest, and that judges don't build their reputations and improve their chances for elevation to a higher court by making huge fee awards, I tried to give Judge Gleeson maximum flexibility to make this determination and soften any harm to his reputation. I dispatched Eric Green, our mediator, to tell Judge Gleeson that I wanted to file a fee petition that would set out the facts and the applicable legal principles but not request any particular fee. I proposed simply to tell Judge Gleeson, "Here are the facts, here is the law—give us whatever you deem appropriate." Green delivered the message and came back with Judge Gleeson's response. The judge rejected my proposal and directed us to ask for a specific amount.

Faced with Judge Gleeson's directive, we not only gave him all the facts and law to make his decision, but we did things for him that had never before been done to ease a judge's burden and make easier the unpleasant task of awarding a massive attorneys' fee. We spent more than a thousand hours reducing the fees requested by each of the 30 law firms on the merchants' side, including our own. We reviewed every time and expense entry from the 30 firms for the seven years, involving the review of more than 225,000,000 hours of attorney and paralegal work descriptions and more than $19 million in expenses.

We established criteria for reducing the fee and expense requests. We did this based upon instinct, experience and what we thought was fair. We applied these criteria uniformly to C&P and the other 29 firms. We rejected all requests that appeared duplicative. We reduced compensable travel time between various cities to what we considered an appropriate level. We rejected requests that we could not understand, knowing that if we couldn't, Judge Gleeson and his clerks certainly couldn't. We reduced the rates requested for attorney and paralegal work to rates we considered reasonable.

We cut attorney hours in a formula designed to reduce what we considered excessively long days, especially those involving coast-to-coast travel. In this exercise, my hours were cut for numerous days when I traveled to San Francisco and worked through the night; that is, after my drink in the Redwood Room of the Clift Hotel. We also rejected requests to reimburse certain hotel stays, laundry expenses, movies at hotels, office supplies and alcohol. I paid for my own drinks at the Redwood Room. We rejected the charges for many meals, such as charges for meals on days when a lawyer worked fewer than a minimum number of hours.

After we did all this, C&P hired an independent accounting firm, Cornick, Garber & Sandler, to reaudit the bill. They worked for roughly 500 hours, completely rechecking C&P's work and making further reductions consistent with the methodology and rules we had established. The result of all this work was the reduction of the so-called *lodestar* by more than $3 million dollars. The lodestar is simply all the attorney and paralegal hours worked on the case, multiplied by the applicable hourly billing rates. Given Judge Gleeson's decision, this reduction in the lodestar of $3 million-plus saved the class more than $10 million. We also rejected over $700,000 in reimbursement expense requests submitted by the lawyers working for the plaintiffs in the Merchants' case.

After reviewing the precedents, I am unaware of any firm ever doing what C&P did with this bill. I am also unaware of any outside court-retained auditor doing such an extensive scrub. The importance of our review was not so much in saving $11 million, but in protecting the integrity of the process and making Judge Gleeson's tough job easier. For this work, Judge Gleeson neither complimented us nor even noted the extraordinary effort. If he had recognized it in his decision, other judges would likely have come to expect or require this type of review in the future.

On top of the audits, we presented Judge Gleeson with every conceivable case arguably relevant to our record result, whether the fees awarded in these cases were high or low. We also submitted the reports of the two preeminent experts in the area of attorneys' fees, Professor John Coffee of Columbia and Professor Arthur Miller of Harvard. These guys had written the book on fees. Arthur Miller was the principal author of the definitive and influential report on attorneys' fees issued several years earlier by United States Court of Appeals for the Third Circuit.

Professor Miller's report in the Merchants' case said:

> "Because there never has been an antitrust class action as complex, as risky, and as hard-fought that has led to similar beneficial results for the class and the public at large, no reported decision concerning a mega-fund case actually can serve as a 'benchmark' for appraising this fee and expense application."

Professor Coffee told Judge Gleeson:

> "[T]his case presents the clearest example that I have ever seen of a 'you-bet-your-firm' case in which the principal law firm that carried this case forward for plaintiffs for over six and one half years of uncompensated litigation was forced to risk its survival; as a firm on the outcome of a single, very high-risk case. Although I have testified in several dozen large class actions regarding fee awards, I have encountered no other case in which the principal law firm devoted the majority of its attorneys' hours over several years to the prosecution of a single action on a contingent fee basis. Indeed, I would have doubted that any firm could have accepted such a level of risk. Here, however, one firm did, persisting over six years and finally achieving not simply an exemplary recovery, but a record one."

Professor Harry First, who is a professor of Antitrust Law at NYU and was Chief of Antitrust Enforcement for New York State, also supported the fee request, stating:

> "I conclude that plaintiffs' counsel did an extraordinary job representing the class in this extremely difficult and highly

risky case. The settlements they have achieved are historic. It is beyond anything that I might have predicted when this litigation was commenced and it is hard for me now to imagine any better result."

The experts who filed these reports all opined that the specific request, that we had reluctantly made, was justified. They organized their analyses around the six factors that Judge Gleeson said governed his determination and "compels the award of an extraordinary fee."

These six factors are:

(1) The time and labor expended by counsel to litigate the case;

(2) The magnitude and complexities of the litigation;

(3) The risk taken by the lawyers who litigated the case on a contingent basis;

(4) The quality of the representation of the plaintiffs;

(5) The relationship of the fee to the settlement; and

(6) The so-called public policy factor, where a court considers whether the fee award will persuade or dissuade lawyers from bringing similar cases in the future.

Judge Gleeson agreed with the experts that on each of these factors, the Merchants' case and the performance of their lawyers was unprecedented. For example, on the first factor, "time and labor," Judge Gleeson said that counsel had

"litigated this case—which did not culminate in settlement until the eve of trial—for seven years. During that time, there were almost 400 depositions of witnesses, including 21 experts who issued 54 expert reports; four rounds of class certification briefing (through the Supreme Court); 16 summary judgment motions, 31 motions in limine and three *Daubert* motions; and a pretrial order identifying 230,000 pages of trial exhibits, 730 trial witnesses, and more than 17,000 pages of deposition designations."

On the second factor, "case magnitude and complexity," Judge Gleeson said the case had been "enormous," involving "almost every U.S. bank and more than five million U.S. merchants."

On the third factor, "risk," Judge Gleeson agreed with Professor Coffee that the case forced plaintiffs' counsel, and especially C&P, to accept an unprecedented level of risk, noting that "Constantine & Partners devoted 52% of its attorney and paralegal resources to this case....[s]uch a hardship weighs in favor of higher compensation, particularly where, as here, Lead Counsel did not benefit from any previous or simultaneous government litigation." Judge Gleeson noted that, unlike many private antitrust cases, "the government piggybacked on Class Counsel's efforts."

On the fourth factor, "quality of representation," Judge Gleeson said:

"The excellence of the representation of plaintiffs, especially in light of the very high quality of opposing counsel, cannot be seriously debated. Constantine & Partners is a premiere plaintiffs' litigation firm, specializing in antitrust litigation particularly, and complex commercial litigation generally.

Its work is uniformly excellent, and thus it is no surprise that it has led the effort that produced the largest antitrust settlement ever."

Discussing the fifth factor, "the relationship of the fee to the settlements," Judge Gleeson said that "the settlements are so large, particularly considering the injunctive relief, that even the exorbitant fee

I award seems small in comparison." That's the way it seemed to us. We believed that the fee we requested was appropriate in comparison to the results we produced. Inasmuch as Judge Gleeson said that this was not merely the perception but the truth, why would he call our request "absurd"? Judge Gleeson was not applying the law, but instead applying his own idiosyncratic standards. He was also writing for the Second Circuit, which he knew would once again be reviewing his work product.

Why should the public care? Aside from the experts, who all supported the fee petition, there was also a good deal of public reaction to the Settlement. David Balto, former chief of policy at the FTC, described the Merchants' Settlement in this manner:

> "Once in a generation an antitrust case offers a chance to restructure an industry. Twenty years ago the settlement of the Justice Department suit against AT&T Corp. led to a proliferation of consumer choice, more innovation, dramatically lower prices, and major telecommunications-industry restructuring. The Wal-Mart settlements offer the promise of many of those benefits."

Professor Robert Lande of Baltimore University Law School stated:

> "The nation's merchants recently won a stunning $3 billion antitrust victory against Visa and MasterCard. But the ultimate winners will be consumers.... As eye-catching as the $3 billion settlements are, the future savings to consumers from this case are likely to be even larger, and the new choices even more important."

Even *Credit Card Management*, a banking industry publication that generally adheres to the industry line, understood the significance of the settlements and reported:

> "The retailers obtained in the settlements everything they had sought since the suit was filed more than six years ago. The honor-all-cards policies are now gone. The plaintiffs will be $3 billion richer. And their most important goal, lower card-acceptance costs, was achieved, as both associations are lowering off-line debit interchange by about a third for most of the rest of 2003."

Confronted with all this expert and industry reaction to the Settlement and his own assessment that the case and result were off the charts in terms of difficulty, risk and results, Judge Gleeson awarded the lowest fee as a percentage of recovery of any "megafund" federal antitrust settlement in history, meaning settlements of $100 million or more. Moreover, it was a record low fee without considering the massive injunctive relief, which Judge Gleeson said was more important and should elevate the fee.

Prior to Judge Gleeson's December 19, 2003 decision, there were twelve federal antitrust megafund settlements.

The average fee awarded in these cases was 24.5 percent. Judge Gleeson said he awarded a 6.511 percent fee. This was the lowest fee as a percentage, and slightly above one-quarter of the average megafund fee. Judge Gleeson made this record low award despite recognizing that our case had been the riskiest and most difficult and had recovered more than the combined total recovered in the eight previous highest antitrust settlements in history, without taking into account the massive injunction.

Judge Gleeson said he was awarding a 6.511% fee, but it is obvious that he didn't do what he said. The fee he awarded, *$220,290,160.44,* was exactly 3.5 times the $62,940,045.84 that we submitted as the lodestar in our fee application. You can take the 6.511% that Judge Gleeson said he awarded at face value or conclude, as I have, that he just multiplied the lodestar by 3.5. The favored method of computing an attorneys' fee in the Second Circuit is the percentage-of-recovery method. Judge Gleeson purported to use the method favored by the Court of Appeals. Judge Gleeson could have been candid about his use of the less-favored method and given some justification for using it. That would have been the proper course for a judge of his stellar qualities, who otherwise did his job with great skill.

Judge Gleeson's fee determination also stated his concern for the class, which he said was "not fully informed" and was not "able to negotiate collectively" over the amount of the attorneys' fee. Judge Gleeson knew that C&P had negotiated a fee with fully informed giant retailers who had much more bargaining power than an eight-lawyer firm, our size at the time of the agreement. These giants, including Wal-Mart, are well known for driving a hard bargain. We told Judge Gleeson pointblank that the fee we applied for was well below the fee we had negotiated at arm's length with Wal-Mart, Sears, Safeway, Circuit City and The Limited.

We calculated what applying our fee arrangement with these five retailers would have yielded for the entire class. It yielded an attorneys' fee of roughly $1 billion. We rejected the use of these negotiated fee arrangements as the basis for our request, although case law says that such a fee arrangement, which comes from arm's-length negotiation, should weigh heavily in a court's decision. Beyond that, we told the Big Five retailers we would waive the agreements and collect whatever the court ultimately awarded. In doing this, C&P voluntarily agreed to collect millions of dollars less from these five giant merchants than they had agreed to pay us. Judge Gleeson knew all this but just chose to ignore it.

After reading Judge Gleeson's decision, including all the praise that he had generously showered on the case, the settlement and the performance of C&P, my personal disappointment about the size of the fee was short-lived. The decision was brought to me at the beginning of a family dinner at the Redeye Grill in Manhattan by one of our paralegals, Kevin Potere. By the end of the dinner, I had gotten over it. I got over the amount of the award in less than two hours, but Judge Gleeson's one paragraph of very nasty comments about the "excessive" and "absurd" request still rings in my ears, because they were so unfair and delivered by a judge who knew better.

I never thought about asking John Gleeson to reconsider his fee award, but I wanted him to change that brief passage in his decision. I wrote to him asking for reconsideration of the wording only in this single paragraph of his 37-page opinion. The letter was short, polite and deferential. My letter gently reminded him of the fact that through the mediator Eric Green, we had told him that we didn't want to ask for any specific fee and proposed that the matter be left totally to his discretion.

In an order worded as if it were a responsive letter to me, Judge Gleeson denied my request to change the language. He implicitly chastised me for not being able to take his criticism but excused me because I probably didn't have the "callouses" he had developed "after two decades of Brooklyn litigation." He reminded me of how "frequently" and "lavishly" he had expressed his "admiration for the forensic abilities, the ethics and the good faith of all the attorneys."

Closing Statement

―――――

WHEN I BEGAN writing this book in November 2003, I predicted that the Merchants' case would not really be over for many years. That prediction proved accurate. As I write these closing thoughts five years later, work on the case continues. For the first two years, we were busy with constant disputes over interpretations of various provisions, appeals of the Settlement and Judge Gleeson's attorneys' fee award and attempts by some merchants, who had excluded themselves from the Class, to belatedly claim some of the money.

Among the group of merchants, who were never in the class or who had excluded themselves but had second thoughts, were AT&T Wireless and the United States, which accepts plastic cards for payment at various facilities. We blocked the phone company's efforts, because acquiescing in its request might have opened up the settlement fund to a larger group of merchants who wanted to have it both ways.

Coming along even later, in March, 2006, was the United States, in a category by itself. In 2002, almost a year before the Settlement, the United States had stated it was not a class member, could not be one and had the right to bring its own antitrust lawsuit against

Visa/MasterCard for money damages. However, during the George W. Bush years, the federal Antitrust Division lost its will to enforce the laws that protect competition, even on behalf of itself. So, the parties acquiesced in Uncle Sam's plea for some settlement money after a round of preliminary fighting. Let's call it our small contribution to a "bailout package" for the federal government.

In January 2005, the United States Court of Appeals for the Second Circuit upheld Judge Gleeson's approval of the Settlement and his award of more than $244,000,000 in attorneys' fees and costs. The decision included lavish praise for the result, its historic significance and our efforts in achieving it, while still approving Judge Gleeson's fee award, a record high in absolute terms, and a record low as a percentage of the result achieved. Appellate judges are generally protective of their lower court colleagues, even when they disagree with the lower court's opinion. The Second Circuit's carefully worded affirmance, written skillfully by Judge Richard Wesley, did not criticize Judge Gleeson but tellingly ended with as much of an apology to lawyers receiving almost a quarter of a billion dollars in fees as is ever likely to be given by overworked judges earning $179,000 a year. The final paragraph of Judge Wesley's opinion concerning the fee award states:

> "A final word is in order here. Measuring the difficulties of a large antitrust action and the degree of success by counsel in forging a settlement is not an easy task. In our view the district court carried out its responsibility with admirable care and thoroughness, and with an eye to a just result. There is no doubt the case dominated the lives of all involved for many years. In approving the district court's fee award, we recognize the sacrifice and commitment plaintiffs' counsel made to its clients while preserving as much as possible for those who were harmed."

In 2005, Constantine & Partners became Constantine Cannon, opening a Washington, D.C., office headed by our former client Steve Cannon. Steve was the General Counsel of Circuit City, one of the lead merchants in the case. Throughout the case, Steve, a leader in the antitrust bar, had the respect of the other powerful outside general counsel in our client group. He was able to explain to them what C&P was attempting to do and why it was taking so damn long. Steve enjoyed and admired the Merchants' case enough to leave what was then a safe and lucrative position for the rough and tumble of high-stakes litigation.

In November 2006, I took a leave of absence from Constantine Cannon to co-chair the transition of New York Governor-Elect Eliot Spitzer, reprising the role I had played as chair of his 1998 transition to Attorney General. The leave became "permanent," or so I thought, when Eliot appointed me his Senior Advisor in early 2007. When Judge Gleeson read about the appointment, he called to congratulate me. Judge Gleeson knew that I had been highly critical of him in a brief to the Second Circuit, supporting the judge's settlement approval, but objecting to the fee award and the language it was couched in. He made the congratulatory call anyway, showing both his tough skin and generosity of spirit.

The Merchants' case has reshaped the industry, but not necessarily in ways that could have been predicted by any of the litigants while it was being fought out. The prices paid for Visa and Master-Card signature debit card transactions declined significantly after the Settlement. The price decreases came in two forms. For all merchants, there was a substantial, but not huge, price drop. The price drop was larger at Visa than MasterCard. Visa had, and has, much more debit card transaction volume than MasterCard. For reasons we understood two decades ago, debit cards will soon overtake credit cards in all meaningful categories. The deep economic recession has merely accelerated the dominance of debit, as people must now pay for things with money they actually have.

For a smaller group of very large merchants, perhaps the top 100-or-so store chains in the U.S., the debit card prices dropped a lot more than the lowered "list prices." Many of these merchants, led by Wal-Mart, threatened to stop accepting Visa and MasterCard debit card transactions unless they got prices much lower than the already decreased prices that the associations adopted in early 2004 as a response to the Settlement. Visa and, separately, MasterCard, negotiated these lower rates individually with each of these very large merchants. Many of these deals included lower prices, not only on Visa and MasterCard debit transactions, but on their credit card and PIN debit transactions as well. Wal-Mart's deals lowered that chain's transaction costs by an amount publicly estimated to be upward of $10 billion in just a ten-year period.

The total amount of all these posted and privately negotiated price decreases over the decade is unknown at this time but likely will be comfortably in the range, predicted by the court, of $25–$87 billion during just that period.

Still, the merchants could have saved and gained even more, had they exercised the same discipline in victory as they did during the long litigation. By and large, they quickly forgot their resolve during the case to stop accepting Visa and MasterCard debit transactions unless the prices dropped even more. Only Wal-Mart and the other 100-or-so large merchants made good on that threat, and only they and their customers will get the full benefit of that resolve. Taking an analogy from my early days as a civil rights lawyer, you can win the right to vote for people who have been disenfranchised, but it's up to them to exercise those rights at the polls. The good news is that those small and medium-sized merchants perpetually have that "right to vote" hard fought and won in the Merchants' case.

Another important result of the case was the wedge it drove between the once inseparable Visa/MasterCard. The finger-pointing and recriminations that began in the weeks after their summary judgment fiasco intensified after the Settlement, as each association scrambled to raise the money necessary to pay the more than $3 billion in cash required. Surprisingly, Visa had the tougher time convincing its banks to bail it out and came very close to going bankrupt. MasterCard had a somewhat easier time, although it made a publicly reported appeal to the European banks of Europay, with which it had merged.

All of the Visa/MasterCard banks were unhappy, and lawsuits started to fly. In one, TCF, a large Midwest bank, sued Visa over the terms of the Settlement, which required Visa and its banks to lower their rates while requiring these banks to effectively advance additional money to Visa so that it could pay for the Settlement. Visa adopted an exit penalty called the "Settlement Service Fee" to prevent its banks from dropping out of Visa and thus avoid paying their "fair share" of the Settlement. Prior to the Merchants' case, there had been sporadic antitrust litigation by financial institutions trying to force Visa to admit them as members. The 1991 *Mountain West* case was one these. After the Merchant's settlement, Visa had to erect barriers to thwart banks from jumping the Visa ship. MasterCard then sued Visa, claiming that this exit penalty was an antitrust violation. The day that pleading was filed was a great day for antitrust law. Visa and MasterCard, formerly united in conspiracy, were now divided in defeat and began to really compete, using the legal weapons that real competitors use against each other.

Although it is arbitrary to designate any one day or event for this honor, and the result that has come to pass, I believe that the day when MasterCard sued Visa was the day the Visa/MasterCard bank cartel breathed its last.

In the wake of the Merchants' Settlement, well over a hundred new class actions were filed, driven by lawyers attempting to hit it big, as they thought we had. And while none of these cases seems to have either the legal talent, the client commitment, or the other attributes that formed the basis of our victory, the amount of money claimed in those cases, still pending against Visa and MasterCard, is in the hundreds of billions of dollars.

In addition to those hundred-plus class actions, two important new individual cases were also filed against Visa and Master-Card—one by American Express and one by Morgan Stanley's Discover Card Network. These cases were the grandchildren of the Merchants' case. I and my firm assumed a primary role in this follow-on litigation.

As Judge Gleeson and the Second Circuit explained in their opinions, the United States' case against Visa/MasterCard "piggybacked" on the discovery and legal and economic theory earlier developed in the Merchants' case.

The U.S. case focused on allegations, first made in the Merchants' case, that Visa/MasterCard had pummeled competitors American Express and Discover, using anticompetitive rules to marginalize those competing card networks. The Shark predicted that Judge Gleeson would invalidate Visa's rule. However, with our help, the U.S. got to trial first and invalidated those particular Visa and MasterCard rules targeting Amex and Discover.

After the U.S. case was successfully concluded, Amex and Discover auditioned counsel and prepared to file suit to collect monetary damages that the court found those networks had suffered, but without specifying the amount. I entered a beauty contest to be Amex's lead counsel but lost out when the starstruck financial services giant hired the legal giant David Boies. I then accepted the offer of Morgan Stanley to be lead counsel for the Discover Card's lawsuit. Morgan

Stanley's then CEO, Phil Purcell, had been in the audience for my 2002 "Dance of Death" speech in Brussels and had not forgotten how I made detailed predictions about the coming final year of the Merchants' case and made good on those predictions.

The Amex and Discover cases were coordinated for most purposes in coordinated proceedings before a single judge, Barbara Jones. Judge Jones had presided over the United States' case against Visa and MasterCard. In these new coordinated cases, Boies and I faced new counsel hired by Visa/MasterCard to replace the huge law firms tiny C&P had routed in the Merchants' case. Visa hired John Keker, a famous San Francisco–based trial practitioner, and Master-Card retained Simpson Thacher, a firm that had been brought in at the conclusion of the Merchants' case, to negotiate an honorable surrender for MasterCard.

These new cases, though very large, should have been straightforward and brief collection actions. All the key facts and legal conclusions had previously been developed in the Merchants' and U.S. cases. A quick victory was my expectation as Boies, Keker, Kevin Arquit (who had moved to Simpson Thatcher) and I argued the major pretrial motions prior to my departure to join the Spitzer administration. As expected, though much more slowly and painfully than warranted, the Amex and Discover cases settled after two more grueling years, in 2008, with Visa and MasterCard agreeing to pay more than $7 billion to the plaintiffs.

Considering both the cash and the more significant and valuable structural and injunctive relief granted in these three cases, the Merchants' case, the Amex case and the Discover case are, in order, the three largest antitrust settlements in U.S. history. But one ironic effect of the Merchants' Settlement was to make it much easier for Visa and MasterCard to pay for the Amex and Discover settlements than the earlier Merchants' payout. That is because the networks were awash with cash as a result of the IPOs they both launched in the wake, and as a result, of the Merchants' case.

In August 2005, MasterCard announced that it would abandon its status as a membership corporation owned by the banks and offer its stock to the public. Visa was later forced to follow suit, reversing the historical trend of MasterCard reluctantly following, or being forced by the banks to follow, Visa's lead. These IPOs were wildly successful, providing the networks enough cash to pay for all three multibillion dollar antitrust settlements. The IPOs are also an effort to place an obstacle between the banks and any future antitrust judgments that might result from the hundred-plus class actions, claiming hundreds of billions, all filed because of our success in the Merchants' case.

With Visa and MasterCard (no longer Visa/MasterCard) converted to public companies, their ability to coordinate and conspire will become even more severely limited than it became after the Merchants' Settlement. The competition between Visa and MasterCard, the additional competition provided by the recently unshackled American Express and Discover, and the innovation that will occur in a newly competitive environment are likely to produce benefits to the public that will far surpass even the record-setting benefits explicitly required by the Merchants' Settlement. That is the way competition and well-crafted antitrust remedies are supposed to work, and once in a generation do.

The Merchants' case had its antecedents in the nonpartisan and collective efforts of state antitrust enforcers to fill the void created when the Reagan administration decided that the antitrust laws had outlived their usefulness. That same spirit motivated the massive dismantling of regulatory supervision at numerous agencies that began under President Reagan and reached full and tragic fruition under President George W. Bush.

In 2005, I served as the keynote speaker at The Federal Reserve's

International Payments Policy Conference in Santa Fe, New Mexico. At 7:00 AM on the morning of May 5, 2005, a contingent of three officials from the Kansas City Fed, who had received a copy of my prepared remarks, knocked at my hotel room door. When I invited them into my room, they asked me to change my speech. They implored me to remove some of my harsh criticism of the Fed's abdication of its role to supervise America's payment system and its laissez-faire attitude toward banks that were pillaging American merchants and consumers. I told these Fed officials that I would reconsider the tone, though not the substance, of the speech they had invited me to give as the keynote speaker of their conference. For the courtesy I gave them by toning down the speech, these Fed officials later rewarded me by refusing to publish an article, on the same subject, that they had solicited from me. The article was later published in two forms by the business schools at Columbia and New York University.

My speech delivered later that day to the Fed conference reported the evolving results of the Merchants' case. I said that the case showed why the Fed should use its existing powers to supervise the American payment system, as it did beginning in 1914, during a period of rapid expansion of interstate commerce. The Fed officials in the audience were polite, but taking my advice was not in the cards for a Fed led by Chairman Alan Greenspan. Mr. Greenspan understood "irrational exuberance" but failed to see that unqualified trust in market forces is also irrational when the market has been distorted by monopoly and market power—which result from lax antitrust enforcement.

As I conclude this book, the Obama administration is in formation. One promise it has made is to revitalize federal antitrust enforcement. Another is to revive regulation and regulatory oversight where it is truly needed. The Obama team, therefore, takes office with opportunities, demonstrated by the Merchants' case, at both the Fed and the federal antitrust agencies.

As of the end of 2008, four waves of settlement checks had been sent to the merchants in the class. Some of those checks are small, but many are in the thousands, tens of thousands, hundreds of thousands, millions, or tens of millions of dollars. Every member of the class who has filed a claim form has been paid the full amount of their signature debit and credit card claims. After that, PIN debit claims will be paid. Then additional checks will be sent to the same claimants from money left over, due to the fact that not all eligible class members filed claims. With each check that is sent, there is a note from Constantine Cannon reminding the merchant why it is receiving the money and how it has benefited and can benefit from the more important injunctive relief that is permanent. The note also thanks merchants for staying the course in the historic case against the now defunct Visa/MasterCard bank cartel.

Oh yes, finally in July 2005, two months after the Supreme Court declined to hear the Merchants' case for the second time, the lawyers got paid. This was almost nine years after the case was filed and more than 14 years after I began preparing it.

A lot of people received a lot of money that July day—in many cases, the biggest payday they will ever experience. That certainly was true at our law firm. Payday included every person in the firm's New York office, including, lawyers, paralegals and clerical and administrative staff. Many of these people did not work on the case, and others actually joined the firm after the case settled. I wanted it to be a nice day for everybody who worked there.

The payment to me was especially large, though not nearly as large as many people believed or continue to. Luckily, coming to me at the age of 58, the money did not do any permanent damage. Some ephemeral and superficial things changed for the worse, and some for the better. On the negative side, I got to experience a shift in the way some people related to me. Up until payday, people who sought me out usually did so for some skill or knowledge they thought I possessed. After payday, I was deluged with the crudest appeals for money. I got personal calls from presidential candidates whose staffs maintain a list of people who are perceived to have the money and the inclination to give it away. Causes came out of the woodwork, often with strident reminders of my responsibility to them. On the positive side, Jan and I were able to increase our support for people and causes we really believed in. We took several dream trips, purchased a few luxuries and then went back to a life remarkably similar to the life we lived prior to payday—and a very good life it was, and is.

With the closing paragraphs of this book, I have also reached emotional closure on this "Great Auk's Egg" of a case, borrowing a phrase from Ford Maddox Ford about his proudest and longest literary work. I think that I understand why I undertook the Merchants' case, why it was successful and what it means to me. We tell ourselves stories about who we are, and why we do things. Sometimes an event provides insight into whether those stories are true. The truth is that I needed this case. I am the son of a brave woman and a brave man, who was also a great athlete. I don't have my father's athletic ability or either of my parents' courage. But they left something in me that compels me to stretch what I have toward their example.

The Merchants' case required me and my colleagues at C&P to stretch way beyond the former boundaries imposed by our limited skills of organization, diplomacy and advocacy. From the outset, it felt like an epic athletic contest. My father, who was also a WWII hero, and other real soldiers who faced real bullets, will forgive my frequent use of military metaphors. I used them because the case also felt like a long war to me.

The Merchants' case gave me what I needed, but it was useful for me to have that assumption confirmed. At the moment that I realized I would eventually receive enough money that I never had to work again, I also realized that I must continue working. I thought that I needed to win the case. Though I'm very happy that we won, as I am happy about the money, I didn't really need the victory. I needed the game, the battle and the stretch. I needed to have a case in which we needed to do, and did, everything. I needed the work.

When John Stockton, the great Utah Jazz point guard, retired in 2003, he was asked whether he regretted never having won an NBA championship. He said he had no regrets and recounted some moments from his long and heroic career. These weren't memories of the playoff finals or even games where he set any of his many personal or league records. They we obscure moments of team solidarity and quiet moments of nonquantifiable personal accomplishment. They occurred in the third quarter of some long-forgotten game in a city that lost its NBA franchise long ago. Stockton said that the part of basketball that he would remember, treasure and build upon in his future was "the journey."

I will remember the Movie Nights at C&P, the trips to Bentonville, Pleasanton, Columbus, Richmond and Hoffman Estates. I will remember my ritual drinks in the Redwood Room of the Clift Hotel in San Francisco, followed by all-nighters. I will remember my tough band of clients incarcerated in a Brooklyn courthouse. I will remember lying in a king sized bed with Bob Begleiter, Mitch Shapiro and George Sampson in the Brooklyn Marriott at 4:45 AM on April 28, 2003, after MasterCard capitulated, and the moment 60 hours later when Visa did the same. I will remember the countless preparation sessions for court appearances and for the trial that never occurred. Many late nights after a long rehearsal, a good one, we would go back to the bottom of the hill and do it all over again, just like Lance. I will remember the journey.

L.C.

December 2008

ACKNOWLEDGMENTS

BEYOND BEING THE reason for my life, and for virtually everything worthwhile in it, my family deserves thanks for helping me with this book and the work it chronicles. Each made important contributions. My wife, Jan, the first and best antitrust lawyer in our home, taught me explicitly and by osmosis and was my advisor on the case and the manuscript. She was the Penelope I returned to after this Odyssey.

My son, Isaac, is the truly talented writer in our family and also a professional editor. His tough, concise, but loving complete edit of the manuscript improved it immeasurably. He also gave the book its title. My daughter, Sarah, worked on the Merchants' case as a paralegal, doing a skillful analysis demonstrating the lack of competition between Visa and MasterCard. She also accompanied me to Amsterdam for work on the case with European merchants and bankers. Elizabeth, our youngest, completed our family and gave a jolt to all our efforts. It is not coincidental that this work began right after her arrival. She accompanied me to Brussels, helped me with the "Dance of Death" speech to the European bankers and told me to "go for it."

Kaplan, my publisher, took a chance on a 62-year-old first-time author. Two people there provided guidance and assistance with the final manuscript. Dedi Felman, my editor, along with my son, took a guy who loved to write and started to turn him into an author. My sessions with Dedi were among the best classes I've ever attended. Don Fehr, Kaplan's editorial director, was the Greenlight and the overall shepherd of this book.

Many of the greatest influences in my life and in this case are mentioned in the book, but one is not—my legal mentor, John Chipman "Chip" Gray. More than anyone, Chip taught me to be a litigator, and by his example, one with a social conscience.

Three women typed the manuscript, fixed my grammar and punctuation, and cheered the old man on in the case and the book. They are Evelyn Maldonado, Mamie Mellerson and Melanie Martorell.

Many of the people in Constantine & Partners, now called Constantine Cannon, are mentioned in Priceless as the key events are discussed, but not all. Many unnamed, who shall remain that way because of their number, did superb and important work. A few, however, will be mentioned. If I was Ferrante, then Michelle Peters was Teicher in the case and in writing this book. A team of six paralegals became C&P's angels of mercy, especially in the crucial endgame year. Alison Ross, Kevin Potere, Kristin Uscinski, Jason Lipton, Michelle Kennedy and Lauren Harrison were so smooth and proficient in their seemingly effortless coordination that I called them the "Boston Celtics"—those of the Cousy, Sam Jones, Sharman, K.C. Jones, Russel era.

C&P's direct clients in the Merchants' case, the Big Five retailers and the three trade associations, placed their faith in an eight-lawyer firm to challenge the banking industry and their law firms with an army of attorneys. They were great teammates, counselors and friends throughout and to this day.

Finally, I want to acknowledge and thank my worthy and skillful adversaries, among them lawyers who were before, or during the Merchants' case became, friends and still are. Patton needed Rommel. Rafa needs Roger. I needed them.

L.C.

N.Y.C.

Index

_____